Moving pictures

Realities of voluntary action

Duncan Scott, Pete Alcock, Lynne Russell and Rob Macmillan

The POLICY PRESS

First published in Great Britain in May 2000 by

The Policy Press
34 Tyndall's Park Road
Bristol BS8 1PY
UK

Tel no +44 (0)117 954 6800
Fax no +44 (0)117 973 7308
E-mail tpp@bristol.ac.uk
http://www.bristol.ac.uk/Publications/TPP

© The Policy Press and the Joseph Rowntree Foundation 2000

Published for the Joseph Rowntree Foundation by The Policy Press

ISBN 1 86134 233 0

Duncan Scott is Senior Lecturer in Social Policy, Department of Social Policy and Social Work, University of Manchester, **Pete Alcock** is Professor of Social Policy and Administration, Department of Social Policy and Social Work, University of Birmingham, **Lynne Russell** is Research Associate, Department of Social Policy and Social Work, University of Manchester and **Rob Macmillan** is Research Student, Department of Geography, University of Durham.

The **Joseph Rowntree Foundation** has supported this project as part of its programme of research and innovative development projects, which it hopes will be of value to policy makers, practitioners and service users. The facts presented and views expressed in this report are, however, those of the authors and not necessarily those of the Foundation.

The statements and opinions contained within this publication are solely those of the authors and contributors and not of The University of Bristol or The Policy Press. The University of Bristol and The Policy Press disclaim responsibility for any injury to persons or property resulting from any material published in this publication.

The Policy Press works to counter discrimination on grounds of gender, race, disability, age and sexuality.

Cover design by Qube Design Associates, Bristol
Front cover: image supplied with the kind permission of the Philadelphia Museum of Art
Printed in Great Britain by Hobbs the Printers Ltd, Southampton

Contents

Acknowledgements

Our greatest debt is owed to the men and women, workers and volunteers, in eight voluntary agencies. They have given us their time and their reflections on numerous occasions, some over a period of six or seven years. We are frustrated because our convention of anonymity precludes a list of their real names. Nevertheless a big 'Thank You' to:

- Counselling Forum
- Family Friends
- Health Self Help
- Kids-Care
- Local Care
- London Ethnic Support Services
- Money Advice Service
- Safety Works

The fieldwork and writing of the agency chapters were undertaken by Lynne Russell and Rob Macmillan.

The report was compiled and managed by Duncan Scott and Pete Alcock.

The interpretation of the research data, and the conclusions drawn, reflect the views of the authors and are not necessarily shared by the agencies involved in the study.

Preface

Despite the growing significance of the voluntary sector in policy planning at the end of the 20th century, and despite the increased research into the size, shape and structure of the sector, we still know relatively little about its everyday dynamics. This report is a plea for a particular kind of qualitative research, which we call 'case study' work – a more issue-based and analytical approach than the more usual, and relatively descriptive, 'case history'. We are hopeful that case study work in general, and this report in particular, can contribute to an improved understanding of how voluntary agencies are structured and evolve, how they respond to, or resist, opportunities and constraints.

The audiences for the report will include:

- policy makers, funders and statutory purchasers who need to understand processes and dynamics (the dimensions of sustainability) as well as structure and output;
- manager practitioners in voluntary agencies seeking to respond creatively to the tensions and contradictions of their work, particularly as expressed in audit and regulatory frameworks;
- workers, volunteers and users concerned to present their needs and capacities as legitimate building bricks in the face of increasingly regulatory and managerial regimes;
- researchers and students attempting to make their activities sensitive to the dynamics of particular contexts, and endeavouring to make sense of their findings in a critically analytical way.

The purposes and potential of the case study approach

"Last year social services announced an across-the-board cut in voluntary sector funding – just weeks before the end of the financial year. There was an angry response from voluntary agencies in the city who, for the first time, lobbied collectively. The outcome was the setting up of a sub-committee involving senior politicians, senior officers from all departments and voluntary sector representatives – to establish a corporate strategy on voluntary sector funding. As a result there will be clearer, more open procedures for funding. Everyone will use the same process.

"The final meeting ... to put the last details together, was held in our offices here. After everyone had left, one of the local authority officers ... hung back.... 'The Chair wants us to put together costings for extending your service...'

"I think to myself 'How dare I represent the voluntary sector in meetings about cuts ... while we are getting such an increase!'" (Senior coordinator, 'Family Friends'*)

* A pseudonym, as are all agency and individual names.

Introduction

A single event or short sequence of events may illuminate some of the issues and contradictions which beset voluntary sector managers (and, no doubt, their colleagues in the public sector). But a flood of subsequent questions can just as quickly threaten any momentary insight. Can we be sure that the perspective has been obtained from a useful vantage-point, and is not just one person's narrow view? How typical is it really? All complex, formal, interorganisational systems must, surely, exhibit such behaviour?

We believe that a case study approach can provide useful material to assist our understanding of the dynamic and contradictory processes at work in voluntary associations and organisations. We also believe that many aspects of these processes could not be explored through more quantitative methods such as the survey, or through more generic qualitative work such as direct structured interviewing.

Of course, we recognise both the strengths and the weaknesses of the case study approach. It can be long-winded, parochial, subjective, full of ambiguous and contradictory material. Yet, at the same time, it confronts and explores difference and complexity in ways which move beyond normative description. It accepts uncertainty and incompleteness, but thereby opens up the possibility that policy makers and practitioners can be helped to better understand voluntary action.

Our work is also in contrast to the challenge posed by Sanger in his discussion of the dehumanisation of many processes of modern policy practice:

We are in an age of rationalism where economic criteria dominate educational ideals, where training philosophy and the managerial imperative would exert greater influence by the day upon the complex life of the workplace. Where every human act is reduced to competency and skill. (Sanger, 1996, p 103)

Those engaged in the day-to-day activities of sustaining voluntary organisation do not experience all human acts just as the exercise of competency and skill – and voluntary organisation – would not survive and prosper if they did. What we hope to reveal through case study analysis is that it is the confusion, complexity, commitment and constancy of voluntary action that characterises the real experience of those involved within it. Through greater understanding of these experiences, others can also learn about the strengths and weaknesses of voluntary action.

In this first chapter, however, it is important to do four things:

- introduce the distinction between 'case histories' and 'case studies', and outline the project upon which this report is based;
- briefly discuss key issues in case study data collection and analysis;
- identify who benefits from a case study approach;
- preview the structure and content of the report.

The case studies project

The aim of this small-scale project was to use case study analysis to explore the issues with which voluntary organisations wrestle on a daily basis. The most common form of 'case study' research on voluntary action consists of detailed accounts of single groups, agencies or locations. Although some of these do include reflective or analytical material, and may work inductively towards explanation, many are largely descriptive and would be better defined as 'case histories'. While both approaches might examine voluntary action through a microscope rather than a telescope, 'case studies' are explicitly concerned with explanatory issues and themes from the outset:

... the case history gives prominence to the story and the story line ... whereas in the case study the story is subordinated to abstract purpose. (Glaser and Strauss, 1967, p 183; see also Plummer, 1983, p 107)

We selected just eight voluntary organisations for investigation. Through lengthy individual interviews we then sought to identify particular incidents which could provide a lens through which to consider more closely eight key themes (listed at the end of this chapter), identified from prior understanding of the issues facing local voluntary activity.

Case study work of the depth undertaken with these agencies was only possible within the limited time-scale and budget of the project because we were able to draw on recent research experience, personal knowledge and contacts, accumulated from a number of previous studies on different aspects of voluntary activity, particularly volunteering and funding (eg Russell and Scott, 1997; and Alcock et al, 1999). These other studies had each involved a relatively small sample of organisations across England, on which we had compiled considerable dossiers of information. The existing knowledge and experience of the research team thus constituted a resource on which this new project could build.

From an initial total portfolio of some 40 case study sites, the eight chosen for further work covered a range of different sizes and structures of associations and organisations, and were selected on the basis that our previous analysis could be built on to explore in more detail each of the eight themes identified by the research team. Contact was re-established with these organisations and further interviews and observations arranged over a three-month period. Our intention was to use organisational boundaries not as ends in themselves, but as the frames within which to identify and analyse issues or themes. As a result of considerable prior familiarity both with the voluntary sector in general, and a cohort of voluntary agencies in particular, we were able to match agency and issue effectively.

We also wanted to produce qualitative material which moved beyond descriptive story telling into a more interpretative issue-based approach. It was anticipated that this would expose intra- and interagency tensions, difficulties and contradictions. Having a long-established relationship with the sample agencies, and having reflected their experiences sympathetically and carefully in the past, was therefore valuable to the research process. This 'closeness' and established relationship, however, also presented a number of methodological problems and challenges to the data collection process which are discussed in the next section.

Data collection and analysis in case study research

The most common form taken by case study research on voluntary action consists of detailed descriptions of single groups, agencies, or locations. Two illustrative collections are:

- First, the 10 abbreviated Master's Degree dissertations published by the Centre for Voluntary Organisation at the London School of Economics. Typical titles are *Birth to five: The establishment of Childline* (O'Connor, 1994) and *The challenge of partnership: A study of the relationship between City Challenge and the voluntary sector in one London borough* (Smith, 1995). Interestingly, although all are marketed as 'voluntary sector case studies', in the words of the editor (Colin Rochester), the methodological detail has been 'ruthlessly' edited away; we learn very little about the case study approach and more about its outcomes.
- Second, a more academically self-conscious collection of case study materials produced from Nottingham University Adult Education Department, under the direction of Konrad Elsdon. Because the central concern of these publications was with processes of learning, there are some glimpses of how the data was collected. The first two studies (Elsdon, 1991) are of a local group of the National Women's Register, which used group interviews and follow-up questionnaires and found the interview work more revealing, and of a local rural community association, which used interviews and researchers' observation to build up a picture of local practice (see also Reynolds et al, 1994).

It is important in this report, however, to give more explicit attention to the methodological issues which arise in undertaking case study research, particularly where such research is driven by analytical themes.

There have been three broad overlapping traditions which utilise case study analysis:

- the researcher attempts to 'fit in' to such social worlds as the school or social work agency, in order to observe, participate and record as closely as possible the perspectives of the principal actors (eg Hammersley and Atkinson, 1996) – the naturalistic or qualitative approach;
- the researcher attempts to use statistical data gathering techniques within a 'case' or bounded setting such as a hospital (eg Yin, 1994) – the quantitative approach;
- the qualitative/quantitative material is used to identify key learning and training issues (eg Heath, 1999; Ritchie et al, 1994; Rochester, 1999; Rochester et al, 1999) – the training approach.

Our research is primarily located in the first of these traditions (see Stake, 1995). It accepts the argument, however, that some of the supposedly sharp distinctions between case studies and other approaches are more apparent than real. There are many design features common to case studies and other research approaches. The differences emerge in the examination of a relatively small number of naturally occurring events and patterns (Hammersley, 1992).

The 'case' in case studies may be an organisation, group or individual; there is no necessary limit to the scale of a case study; a 'bounded study' – in time as well as place – can range from micro social worlds to societal, inter-societal and global levels. Perhaps more creatively, it may even be an incident or event. Instead of concentrating on a story as an end in itself, however, there must be a concern with the extent to which it illuminates single or recurrent events of a formal and informal nature. For example, a formal meeting or informal encounter, an agreement or conflict. Even though such dichotomies are unlikely in 'real' social life, they point towards issues as organising devices, because:

> Issues are problems about which people disagree, complicated problems within the situations and contexts. (Stake, 1995, p 133)

Descriptive case histories emphasise their detail; they involve close observation and discussion, and therefore we can have confidence in them. If all we want are relatively 'thin' accounts, which take much for granted and avoid too much probing beneath surfaces, then all is well. On the other hand, if those responsible for case studies (interviewer and interviewee) are determined to collect data which does go beyond normative accounts about how well the agency is doing, and/or how much better things could be if only X policies and Y resources were implemented, then a degree of awareness or reflexivity is necessary.

'Thick' detail requires attention to:

- the interviewer and modes of data collection;
- the interviewee and the source of their knowledge and understanding;
- the general and particular contexts within which interviewer and interviewee interact.

The research team had to deal with the particular challenges of familiarity. The interviewers already knew their agencies and the initial gatekeepers or interviewees. Thus, even though both parties had some anxieties about the interaction, there was an underlying sense that for both of them the renewed contact provided an opportunity for 'brief therapy':

> "It is probably the case that they do talk to you because they feel buffeted and we may be one of the few external agencies offering to listen – given the necessary boundaries on disclosure to other voluntary organisations or the statutory sector." (Project researcher)

> "Most of the people I interview actually learn quite a lot about *me* in a very short space of time – because along the way they will have it spelled out for them – I'm a woman, I'm middle-aged, I'm a mum.... The downside of this dimension of the relationship is that it makes issues involved in betrayal or misrepresentation all the more critical." (Project researcher)

Some of the interactions therefore felt ill-disciplined as the conversation went off track, but this often proved to be helpful in unexpected ways.

> "Everyone is very different. Some give you important 'revelations' in the midst of talking about stuff you hadn't necessarily wanted them to talk to you about. There is, therefore, a danger in going into the interview with a very fixed set of ideas and a very fixed set of questions. Frankly I think we would have missed half of the findings we have had over the years if we had done that." (Project researcher)

> "If you think about one of our agencies in particular, about their funding dilemma and the coordinator swearing about it – that story came out in the course of her chatting to me about a bad bout of 'flu and coming back to the office to find the application form on her desk. Had we not had a relationship in which she was able to feel comfortable about speaking frankly and expressing anger and frustration in that way, I do not know whether that story would have emerged at all, or been told in the same way – with graphic detail and forcefully expressed feelings and views." (Project researcher)

Familiarity led to the disclosure of dense detail in some instances and not others. For example, one interviewee spoke frankly about internal organisational detail at the first interview, but was evasive, bordering on contradiction, at the second. As it had become clearer that the research project was interested in tensions and interpersonal difficulties within the organisation, so the interviewee became more uncomfortable. Understandably, respondents become defensive and feel vulnerable to the extent that they might then reveal inconsistent personal and organisational behaviour.

Disclosure depends not just on whether the focus is external or internal, but on the relationship between interviewees and the people subject to scrutiny or critique. Some will paint a coherent, 'official view', while others feel confident about acknowledging conflict either because they feel very strong as senior managers ('high-ups') or even because they feel the opposite and so out of control as to be able to 'relax' by talking freely of their grievances ('low-downs'). In short, what people disclose and how they do this partially reflects their status and authority within an association or organisation. Data collection for interviewer and interviewee alike is therefore never an unproblematic, purely technical affair; it is embedded in social relationships which, when revealed, can illuminate and give depth to the case study.

Knowing that interviewees may consciously or unconsciously provide perspectives or points of view partially dependent on their social location in the agency is of heuristic value when making sense of data. But our interviewees are never entirely social constructs in this narrow sense. They also differ in the extent to which they can act as 'story-tellers'. Some people are natural 'gossips', while others commentate in abstractions without ever touching on the people involved. Just because they have been full participants in a set of events does not guarantee an ability to talk about them. Furthermore, the limited time and resource constraints of the project meant that we often could not afford to spend enough time facilitating story telling.

> "We are asking them to do something which is quite difficult to do on the hoof – to call to mind a meeting, an incident, a conversation which encapsulates the issues around a strategic theme. That is a tall order – it assumes that they have consciously analysed the issues for the organisation and can quickly locate those issues in a specific story.

> "Their difficulty in telling a story may equally be a reflection of the difficulty experienced by the interviewer in spontaneously calculating a set of useful prompts!" (Project researcher)

Finally, making sense of the data depends on two sets of tensions. Firstly, the researcher has to 'know' the context of the case sufficiently well to be able to assess how far the details really are illuminating. It is a well-worn adage that many researchers only look for events and issues under the metaphoric street-light where there is enough light; they need to be persuaded that stories as data are relevant to the explanatory task not just because they are 'interesting'. It may therefore be necessary to move away from the physical brightness in order really to 'see'. Secondly, this intellectual task must simultaneously endure the strain between an undoubtedly false goal of perfect representations of reality and the pain of simplification. The compromises inherent in this latter approach are probably the most distressing occupational hazard for the case study researcher for,

> Whatever their purpose, maps and models must simplify as much as they mimic the world. (Sanger, 1996, p 46)

A further challenge for the case study researcher in making material public is to be sensitive in handling what can undoubtedly be awkward truths. 'Awkwardness' is about both intellectual and ethical dilemmas. In the first instance the task for the researcher is to re-present data in such a way that those who provided it are not discouraged, but rather are able to continue as participants in its refinement and dissemination. To further this process, it is argued that

> ... case study presentations should be basically *inconclusive* accounts of what happens.... (Sanger, 1996, p 119; author's emphasis)

We would agree that the degree of conclusion is most significant, as it cannot be assumed that only researchers are able to reach the lofty heights of conclusion. This, of course, is an intellectual (epistemological) and political point of great practical importance, because it recognises that 'ordinary' people have both knowledge and understanding.

The second awkwardness derives from the very relationships which facilitated the dense detail. It is self-evident that the anxieties of interviewees during the early stages of research do not fade away; they are latent and only require the lightest droplets of a published account to rapidly sprout up again. There are no easy escapes for the researcher who wishes to present dense detail within a critical and reflective account, and even those who have strained towards a relatively neutral and so-called 'objective' account have had a difficult reception. For example:

> In trying to be objective in my written account I had avoided using value-laden terms and in *their* view failed to present a positive account of the school....
> (Burgess, 1985, p 192; author's emphasis)

Some of our chapters point up both negative and positive dimensions of voluntary action. We anticipated that our interviewees would recognise themselves and feel alarmed by what they read. Our obligation here is not just a personal or individual one; we must also be sensitive to the potential impact of the research report on interviewees and the agencies for which they work. It is important not to undermine their interpersonal and intraorganisational relationships while analysing the tensions and dynamics inherent in them. It is not unusual perhaps in case study research to create disguises for the participants – by changing agency names, geographical locations or the gender of interviewees. In addition to these devices, however, an important element of our research process has been to consult the interviewees after the fieldwork stage to ascertain:

- whether we have anonymised their organisation sufficiently, and
- whether the account we have given does reflect some of the reality of their experience around the particular theme identified without undermining them, and while accepting that our account may not be the whole story. It is explicitly understood that within each case study organisation there may be other perspectives we have not addressed and developments since the fieldwork about which we are unaware. The concern within each chapter, however, was to capture at least *some* of the concerns and dilemmas voluntary organisations experience in relation to specific themes and to present 'generalisable illustrations'.

A commitment to this careful consultation process was given to participants at the outset of the research. Indeed concern by one agency about the impact of the research on external relationships led to its insisting on a right of veto over inclusion of their story in the report. A compromise was achieved whereby, in the event of concern over the sensitivity of the material in the draft chapter, the researcher and interviewee would work towards achieving a version which was both analytically accurate and protective of the agency's wider long-term interests. In the final event this was not necessary. Although those who commented on the draft chapters did feel discomfort at seeing their feelings, views and experiences printed in such detail, and most sought some minor changes to conceal the organisation's identity (but not their own), all concluded that the overall analysis had captured the essence of the theme for their agency.

"Our first reaction to our chapter was that we were quite shocked – and a bit worried that people would be able to identify the organisation. On the other hand, when we thought more about it, I don't think you should take anything out because it's true. We were amazed that you managed to capture how we were feeling at the time." (Telephone follow-up with case study interviewee)

Who benefits from case studies?

In the particular example of this study clearly we hope that our respondents, both during the data collection and in reading this report, will find themselves helped. We have certainly profited from the detail about processes and relationships which emerged out of the established links made by members of the research team.

Looking more generally, however, to the wider audience for case study work, the primary sponsors of research into voluntary activity are usually government departments, anxious to regulate and evaluate their increasing investments. Not far behind them are managers within the voluntary sector, who are searching in a competitive and audit-driven environment to retain or build their agency position. However, those who potentially have most to gain from case study approaches are workers and volunteers. Greater attention to processes and pressures can underline how systematic are the uncertainties and contradictions, and how they cannot be explained away as the 'fault' of managers and sponsors, workers or volunteers.

A secondary collection of audiences are those who research and study voluntary action, whether as professional purveyors of information and analysis, or as embryonic professionals engaged in learning and training. They too have a part to play in arguing for and implementing a greater plurality of approaches to make sense of voluntary action.

There are some signs that the importance of qualitative research, including case study work, is being increasingly recognised. In September 1999, the Scottish Local Government Information Unit organised a conference on the role of qualitative approaches in the new local government agenda. Contributors warned of the dangers of an over-dependence on statistics and stressed the value of qualitative work in adding to explanation through "... exploration, description, diagnosis and prediction" (Vittles, 1999).

Case study approaches can contribute in two overlapping ways to a more informed understanding of the policy and practice significance of voluntary organisations and volunteers. Firstly, they can contextualise beliefs and behaviour in order that we can more readily appreciate the particular circumstances of an individual, organisation or sector. For example, to be able to observe and discuss the specific dimensions of volunteer 'commitment' (Chapter 3) is to realise that this is often much more mixed or contradictory than we realise. Many people 'soldier on' as much because they are unsure how to exit without offending friends and colleagues in relatively small-scale social worlds as because they are unequivocally 'volunteering' their time. Insights of this kind have consequences for any discussion concerning the promotion or development of volunteering.

Secondly, closer attention to detail can lead to a critical reassessment of behaviour. For example, during the recent discussions about 'Compacts' between government and the voluntary sector there has been much welcome attention to the need for clear, explicit statements about institutional relationships. Yet, even as these various compacts unfold, it is also clear how organisations find themselves (willing or not) enmeshed in more informal relationships with the very same government departments. The 'need' to act quickly in the vanguard of policy initiatives often leads to arrangements outside, and in contradiction to, Compacts and other formal frameworks, as revealed in the vignette which opened this chapter (also discussed in Chapter 9).

The structure and content of this report

The heart of our report consists of eight chapters which present and analyse themes of central concern to the voluntary sector. These are arranged in a sequence which begins with an internal focus and ends with an external one.

In each chapter the theme is illustrated by detail from one voluntary agency. Although the presentation of themes and illustrations necessarily varies, it is contained within a common format: an opening vignette, discussion of the theme, an introduction to the agency context, the analysis, a conclusion and policy implications.

The final chapter (Chapter 10) revisits the purposes and potential of case study research in relation to voluntary action, and explores the implications for such different audiences as policy makers, practitioners, researchers and students.

The eight themes and agencies are thus:

Infrastructure	–	Local Care
Values and identity	–	Health Self Help
Social entrepreneurs	–	Safety Works
Stakeholders	–	Kids-Care
Managerialism	–	London Ethnic Support Services
Strategic planning	–	Counselling Forum
Networking	–	Money Advice Service
External agendas	–	Family Friends

2

Infrastructure

Introducing the theme: infrastructure

The infrastructure of many small to medium sized voluntary organisations is under-resourced. Workers operate in environments which people in other sectors would find unacceptable. Funders are unenthusiastic about paying for improvements to renewable capital – premises, office equipment, transport – and available resources are focused on service delivery at the point of contact with the service user. Yet an inadequate physical infrastructure, together with under-resourced training budgets or management and administrative systems, have implications for the organisation's capacity to deliver services efficiently and (cost) effectively. The resultant unpaid overtime/voluntary activity undertaken by paid workers provides a compensatory subsidy. There is little recognition of the added value from investment in physical and human capital, either by those who fund voluntary organisations or even by some management committees, paid workers and volunteers in the sector itself – those who attach a particular 'traditional' image to voluntary activity and would see such expenditure as being the antithesis of what the voluntary sector is about.

In this chapter we will go behind the doors of just one organisation to demonstrate some of these points; to reveal the 'cracks' or tensions in what are sometimes felt to be the merits of the 'real' voluntary sector – namely its ability to achieve much with very little, and its dependence on its embeddedness in local institutional life. The detail of the account will be unique, but many in the voluntary sector will identify with it.

Introducing the agency: 'Local Care'

Our first visit to 'Local Care', a community care organisation on the Welsh borders, was in 1992. From a shared office at the back of a church hall, and with just one part-time worker and a network of over 150 volunteers, the organisation provided a range of community care services – home visiting, equipment loans, and a voluntary community transport scheme. At that time the focus of our research was the funding of locally based voluntary organisations and the key issues for this agency, over and above the perennial task of raising the bulk of its income from a variety of small grants from charitable trusts, from donations and local fundraising activity, were twofold:

- how to finance the replacement of its minibus, and the acquisition of a second one;
- the loss of its grant from social services; the sum was insignificant – £750 a year – but the cut was symbolic for an organisation which was made to feel small, marginal and undervalued, despite the extent to which its referrals came from statutory agencies.

By the time of our most recent visits in 1999 there had been two important changes:

- annual income had doubled to £20,000; half of this now comes from a recently negotiated three-year contract with social services, with the balance still being found from other sources;
- the long established coordinator had retired and had been replaced by a younger woman – once a volunteer – supported by an administrative worker; both posts are still part time, just 18 hours a week each.

In the past the organisation ran in some respects like a family business. For the previous coordinator and her husband (who at various times was the treasurer and the secretary to the management committee), it was very much part of their domestic world and was cross-subsidised by

their own time and home environment. Indeed when the present coordinator was first appointed as administrative assistant she was surprised to learn that the then coordinator was a paid worker and not a volunteer. Record keeping at the office was relatively unsystematic; accountability to, and control by, the management committee was nominal; the management committee was large (24 members) and unfocused. It included many representatives from other local organisations and individual members, some of whom rarely attended. The office environment was run down. Given its financial context – particularly its dependence on fundraising and donations – there was an understandable culture of 'making do', and in some cases of making false economies, thus:

- the decision that the organisation could not afford a service contract on a photocopier which often went wrong, and
- the personal delivery of committee minutes and newsletters by the coordinator for example.

Many commentators on the voluntary sector will feel an affection for this type of organisation. Some will feel nostalgia for what they might describe as the 'real' voluntary sector – notably those who do not have to struggle with its frustrations or the difficulty of sustaining its work in the long term. The new staff appointed three years ago, however, have brought with them a different ethos from their predecessor:

- They have a clearer demarcation between their working lives and their personal lives – although it remains the case that "every time a management committee member is there as a volunteer, we are too", and they continue to take their turn outside local supermarkets on flag day and at fundraising events.
- They have higher expectations of their working environment both in terms of the physical environment (their accommodation, facilities and equipment) and in relation to their employment rights, their training, management and personal development: "We've just had our first pay slip in three years."
- They want to establish what they describe as more business-like, more 'professional' administrative systems and processes and a more effective decision-making structure.

Some of these changes have in fact been made necessary by the very different legislative and financial environment in which the organisation now works:

- the demands of increased charity regulation, not least in relation to financial accountability;
- increased external accountability and service monitoring as a result of the social services contract and, to a lesser extent, the lease agreement with the local authority for their second minibus;
- the organisation's expanded role.

These changes have had implications for the organisation's administrative systems, management processes, technological requirements and training needs. The change in staffing, however, also means that shortcomings in the organisation's infrastructure are now more likely to be identified as 'problems' and to be articulated by the workers as issues to be addressed, rather than being perceived as inevitabilities. In the following accounts the workers give some flavour of their working environment.

A day in the life of ...

... Jane – the coordinator

"Imagine it's Monday morning. We both have to be here for 8.30am. First of all you have to get everything out – everything had to be put away on Friday so the church could use the room at the weekend. So you've got to put the desks and chairs back into position, pull the computer back to where it should be, take the divert off the 'phone – calls are diverted to me at home at the weekend because sometimes the church switches the power off at 4pm on a Friday – and remember to switch the 'phone back on. (We turn it off not to disturb people who use the room on a Sunday.) Then plug the other phone back in – it has to be disconnected because it won't access the divert. I don't know why.

"On Monday morning you've got to remember to put the wheelchairs through into the church and put the heating on because this is 'Leisure Day'. Sometimes the church invites a speaker, but quite often they have a sing song and we can't hear a thing in here. Once I was on the 'phone to someone and I had to say 'I'm sorry I can't hear you' and she replied – 'Well turn the radio down then!' On the other hand we have to try not to go through and disturb them. So if you need to go to the toilet, you have to try and sit there. Most of the time we manage it – but sometimes you just have to go!

"Then you collect the mail. We're in the process of changing the letter box because we read this sheet that came from Age Concern and we realised that we are open to criticism because the volunteers who go past on a weekend will push donation envelopes from clients through the door, and there's just a wire basket on the other side. So we've asked someone to make us a wooden one with a lock. There will be donation envelopes, post and minibus keys in there.

"Then it gets to 9 o'clock – the two of us sit from 8.30am to 9am without the telephones on because once they start!... Sometimes we start to discuss something at 9am and we don't finish it that day, because the telephone constantly rings and rings. While I arrange visits and transport, Ann will deal with the paperwork and finance. On a daily basis there might be anything from £70 to £450 to count and process."

... Ann – the administration worker

"Yes. If it's been the end of the month and the invoices have gone out to organisations which have hired the minibuses, people still sometimes come in with the cash as against cheques. I can bank up to £300-£400 in cash. When we did the flag day collection there was over £335 in cash and I had to take it home to count which I shouldn't have done. But I knew Jane was going to be away on the Monday and I would be on my own in the office. There was no way I would get it counted then, so I had to do it at home. Also there is nowhere secure in the office where money could be kept. I don't like taking it home – it's a terrible responsibility, especially when it hasn't been checked – but no one else wants to do it. The system is open to criticism and suspicion.

"When I count the money in the office, until a month ago I did not have a proper desk. I had an old kitchen table and to stop the pennies going all over the place – they would either go down the crack or stick to the surface – I had to put a plank of wood across the table. It was an old shelf someone had brought in. But I've now got a proper desk! The way that came about was that I was on the 'phone to one of the Trustees and he said 'Do you still need a computer?' I said 'No – all we do now is beg for desks.' He said 'I'll see what I can do'. That seems to be how things happen – you can ask and ask, and then….."

... Jane (who also needs a new desk) added:

"I saw one on offer in a catalogue so I passed the catalogue to the chairman about a month ago but I haven't had a response. It was about £100. If we've had one given to us, then surely it's not going to break the bank? Everything we've got up until now we've begged and borrowed. We've spent very little on the office – but we're getting better at it."

What would your priorities be if you had a windfall?...

... Jane

"My priority would be accommodation. It is very difficult for Ann to do the finances and paperwork with the 'phone ringing all the time and lots of interruptions by volunteers or service users or people involved with the church. Also if someone comes in who needs to talk – they may have been bereaved and in tears – there is nowhere private I can take them. There are also issues around security and personal safety when one of us is here on their own. If you were in any difficulty, there is no one to help and no alarm system. You have to lock the office door in order to go to the toilet. You feel quite vulnerable in the church at 8.30 on a dark winter morning. The rent at the church has recently gone up but it is still only £500 a year and includes bills. This is the problem – we do really need to move premises but it could eat up the money. We would have to be able to guarantee we could get in the additional money.

"Also I get frustrated sometimes – it's not boring but a lot of the day-to-day work doesn't stretch you – matching volunteers with requests, organising minibus drivers. It's very time consuming – I'm scrabbling around like a rat in a wheel peddling furiously and as soon as I've got one day organised, I have to start again to organise the next. There's such a volume of it, I can't stop doing it to do

anything else. I would like some training in PR and marketing – if someone in advertising, say, could just come and talk to me about ways I could promote the organisation or bring some volunteers in. I have talked to the committee about this – but I don't think they took on board that the coordinator might walk out because she sometimes gets fed up to the back teeth of doing the same things over and over again. Or perhaps I could have just one day a month when I don't come into the office – when I can go out – go round a few GP surgeries and give practice managers our leaflets for example, or organise the minibus training days."

... Ann

"I'd like to understand more on the accounting side with SORPs (Statement of Recommended Accounting Practice by Charities). Everybody keeps talking about it and I keep getting all these sheets. Something came through the post the other day about a training package, but it costs £5,500! It's a computer package and a three-day course! – but I'd just like to be a little bit more aware, as they seem to be taking the responsibility off the Treasurer and putting it into the office."

External relationships: the importance of social infrastructure

The probability of a windfall which would finance these modest ambitions is slight. Even the organisation's social services contract is uncertain beyond the next three years, and made more so by the creation of Primary Care Groups, their relationship with social services and their different geographic boundaries. The avenues through which such voluntary organisations might improve their internal infrastructure, their human and physical resource base, are often through the organisation's wider social infrastructure either by negotiating personal deals or through local networks, as in the following examples:

Basic computer training

"We only use 1% of the computer's capacity – we simply don't know what it can do. Apparently there is a course at the college and it's £35 an hour but there has to be a minimum of 10 people. We don't really want to go to the college – what we want is specific training for what we need. I rang twice and in the end she came back and said they'd agreed to do it, but it would still cost £35 an hour. The Chair put it to Age Concern England who have a scheme to help other organisations – called 'Getting Fit for Funding' – with a budget for training. We're still waiting to hear whether the cost can be covered by that. Otherwise we will not be able to pursue it. When we bought the computer, we had gone to the limit of our budget for it and could not afford the manual. The committee didn't really want to spend more. Instead it'll just cost £1,000 in training!"

Office equipment

"We've now got a 'new' filing cabinet – we did a swap. You've seen the old wooden kitchen cabinet in the office – sort of 1940s or 1950s. Well we had one previous to that – a green one. It was in such a state – and I was telling a friend who has an antique business – and she said she would do a swap for a filing cabinet because the Americans go wild for these cupboards!"

Conclusions and policy implications

What small, successful voluntary organisations lack in financial resources, they often make up for in resourcefulness. It would also be a mistake to 'problematise' their infrastructure to such an extent that the advantages of interdependence between community-based organisations are undervalued – together in this case with the financial benefits, and local accessibility, of their location – the possibility, for example, that volunteers who are 'passing by' can just pop in. There were nevertheless important infrastructure issues here which have implications both at the point of service delivery and for the longer-term sustainability of the organisation. Some of these issues have been exacerbated by the changing demands made on the organisation; by its recent entry into the world of business plans, monitoring and evaluation reports, and the need for systems to demonstrate contract compliance and financial probity.

Clearly there are a number of avenues through which an organisation can improve its physical and social infrastructure, and the capacity and skills of its workers – avenues which rely less on financial resources than on flexibility, imagination

and networking. The case study has signalled the potential importance of personal networks and voluntary sector networks to organisations with limited financial resources. However, one of the constraints on an organisation with relatively few active members on its management committee and a reliance on a small number of employees is its capacity to develop that social infrastructure. It is difficult for workers to network to any significant extent with other organisations when they are already working at full stretch just to organise and administer service delivery. Networking is not only important for workers, socially, psychologically and professionally, but also for the organisation in terms of information, in having a stronger collective voice, and in terms of negotiating partnerships or agency relationships which confer economies of scale, and access to services and facilities or to funding opportunities.

It is important that the trustees of organisations concerned with service delivery and having very limited budgets accept the legitimacy of infrastructure issues. There is also a need for recognition by trustees of their role as employers and their responsibilities in relation to health and safety. It is essential that they recognise the importance of investment both in physical infrastructure and in the workers themselves – acknowledging their development needs and personal goals, and recognising the potential benefits to the organisation of somehow enabling them to participate in local forums and to network with other organisations.

Outside of the organisation itself, it is clear that there is scope for voluntary organisations not only to share accommodation which is more appropriate to their individual and collective needs, but also potential for larger voluntary agencies to provide training, advice and access to facilities which smaller agencies could not afford individually. However, funding agencies, and statutory purchasers who rely on voluntary organisations to provide basic local services, should also recognise the infrastructure needs of voluntary organisations as a legitimate cost. This organisation is small but not marginal – and certainly not to those who benefit from its services. In the first six months of its contract, with just two part-time workers, a team of volunteers and the working environment described here, the organisation met 3,500 service requests – whether for transport, assistance to attend hospital, befriending or shopping.

3

Values and identity

Volunteering has become too much of a distraction

Breezing into the small net-curtained side-room, Bob, the treasurer, by his presence alone, interrupted the proceedings: "What, we giving away prizes this morning or what?!"

He was late for the committee meeting, and the other eight members of the committee were, surprisingly, all gathered around the table listening to the secretary go through her correspondence. He was being a touch unfair. The committee struggles a bit, but most people make it to most meetings. And it was the AGM that afternoon in any case. Anyway it's only Bob, with his usual jokey manner. He was usually very confident and ebullient – he had a background in industry, and was now self-employed.

Correspondence over, it was time for the treasurer's report. The usual stuff about the year gone by, which would be put before the membership that afternoon. Money was generally OK. It was remarkable that over the three or four years that Bob had done the books, the amounts at the end of the year always tended to come out more or less the same. Membership was reasonably steady for the time of year at 120. It usually creeps up to about 170 tops, although there has been a slow decline in members.

"There might be a problem with membership of the committee this year though."

Nobody took the hint, not even the researcher in the corner taking notes. All became clear at the end of Bob's report: "I no longer want to do this next year. It's too much of a distraction. Michael goes to university next year and I need to get some work in. I will continue to support it this year until the committee can get another treasurer."

It went deathly quiet in the room.

How long was the gap before anybody spoke? It's hard to say – maybe 10 seconds, maybe 15. These things tend to get exaggerated, but it was long enough for the researcher to look around to see what would happen next, and then to look down in embarrassment. It's hard to say whether people were too surprised to say anything or just didn't know how best to deal with the situation. Finally the chair spoke, rescuing us all from the silence: "Right. Chairman's report."

Introducing the theme: values and identity

This snippet of reality within a voluntary organisation suggests seemingly endless questions regarding the nature of the organisation, the dynamic interactions, past and present, of the people involved, the consequences of individuals becoming involved and then ceasing to be involved. Why do people join and participate in voluntary organisations? Why do some participate and others not? How do they become involved? Once involved how is that involvement framed, viewed, extended or intensified? Why do people continue being involved? Why and how do they leave groups? These are vital questions for anybody concerned with the vitality and vibrancy of voluntary organisations and the sector overall. Since voluntary endeavour in some guise is a defining feature of the sector, answers to the 'how' and 'why' questions behind decisions to volunteer or not to volunteer, and behind decisions to continue or not to continue volunteering are central to a complete understanding of the rhythms of the sector.

But how are we to begin to address these questions? It is unlikely that a simple explanation of the dynamics of volunteering and voluntarism is possible. Broader contextual explanations of voluntary activity usually refer to the degree of cultural/social maturity, employment status, social group or income levels and educational background. But thinking only of such factors misses the essential dynamic of how and why people volunteer, and how and why they stop volunteering. In particular, how do the values and identities of individuals affect motivations and decisions with respect to volunteering, and conversely how does voluntary activity shape values and identity?

Arguably much of the existing literature in this area, in its concentration on aggregates and survey based measurements of volunteering and 'social capital', misses the nuances and puzzles of everyday voluntary activity. Telling a story of the ordinary practice and rhythm of life within a voluntary group may not provide a comprehensive examination of voluntary activity, but without this richness of detail and depth, an essential element of the reality of voluntarism is likely to be lost. So what of Bob the treasurer's decision to resign? What lies behind all this?

Introducing the agency: 'Health Self Help'

'Health Self Help' is a membership-based self-help group run entirely on a voluntary basis. It was formed in 1979 when a number of people responded to a 'call to arms' regarding a particular medical condition in a newspaper article. A subsequent meeting of interested people in a church hall decided to establish a group to meet on a regular basis. The group's activities are coordinated by a committee of nine members, and it now meets monthly in a couple of rented rooms in a church in the town centre. The committee has its meeting in the morning, in the net-curtained room, after which there is a break for people to have their sandwiches and a cup of tea. Then the focus shifts to a larger hall for the open meeting in the afternoon where ordinary members gather to chat and share experiences and listen to invited speakers. The group also runs a helpline, and publishes a number of leaflets as well as a monthly newsletter circulated to its 170 members. It is affiliated to a national organisation, and often gets involved locally on campaigns developed from a national level.

Financial situation (£)

31 March	Income	Expenditure	Annual balance	Reserves
1997	2,754	3,756	(1,002)	4,677
1998	2,608	2,745	(137)	3,675
1999	2,525	3,120	(595)	3,080

(= deficit)

In the year ending 31 March 1999, Bob reported to the committee that the main sources of income were from annual subscriptions and donations (£964: 38%), two small grants from the local authority (£720: 29%) and sales of a self-help booklet *Helpful hints* (£309: 12%). Bob referred to the fact that sales of the booklet were gradually declining over time – that the market was 'saturated' and that it was on the 'downwave of its product cycle'.

Because the group is completely voluntary, there are no salary costs. The main expenditure items are room hire (£420: 13%), for the two rooms once a month in the church building, affiliation to the national organisation (£485: 16%), and the payment of fees for a couple of specialist courses related to the health condition attended by health service staff (£660: 21%).

Health Self Help is a small organisation, in terms of money, activities and members. There are thousands of similar sized voluntary groups operating at a local level all over the country, doing an astonishing variety of things for their members or for others. They have negligible financial and physical resources, and so their developments and their stories invariably revolve around people who are more or less energetic volunteers. How did they get involved in the first place, and how do they keep going? What happens if someone decides they might wish to be less involved, or even leave?

Values and identity in context

'Getting involved' and 'staying involved'

'Getting involved' in Health Self Help seems to be the result of a combination of unsolicited 'volunteering' as well as different varieties of recruitment – from open requests to more blatant dragooning. Often the processes might be the result of a chance occurrence, or a combination of fortuitous circumstances. Of course a potential volunteer would have to be in the right place, at the right time, and be relatively open to suggestion. As researchers we might have to think of different contextual reasons for explaining why particular people might be (i) in the right place, (ii) at that time and more importantly (iii) open to suggestion.

For voluntary associations finding enough willing and active volunteers is a continual problem. This exchange between Sandra, the secretary, and Margaret, the chairperson, illustrates some of the different views about this:

Sandra: "It could be something to do with people today. Attitudes. Nobody's wanting to do anything. They're all wanting to take. Nobody's wanting to give. And I think it's ...the younger ones ... just don't want to know ... I think it will [affect other groups] in this day and age because it's just a general ... well, attitude, for want of a better word."

Margaret: "I don't think that attitude is so prevalent."

Sandra: "What?"

Margaret: "That not caring."

Sandra: "I'm not saying that they're not caring. They're just not ... they just don't want to get involved."

Frank referred to the strategy of getting people involved by asking individuals directly:

"I think people sometimes ... they don't like to refuse. They've every right to. We wouldn't think any worse of them for it. But I think that's it – they feel as though they're in a can't win situation."

Sandra's increased involvement came through offering her particular services and skills from when she used to work as a school administrator:

"They sent a letter around because the secretary wanted to retire and they couldn't get a replacement and they'd been trying. So they were asking if any members had got, you know, expertise in that field – otherwise they'd have to fold. So I'll be quite honest I gave it a good fortnight to let anybody who wanted to volunteer volunteer. And then I wrote and offered my services ... and so I became secretary. And then got involved and found out more about it...."

Margaret, a founding member who attended the original meetings in the church hall, became the first and still continuing chairperson through what appears to be the embarrassment, and thus pressure, of silence:

"And they wanted a chairman you see. And you know when they want anybody like that it goes deathly quiet and I thought 'Oh no I can't stand this'. Chairman? Well basically it's just a figurehead isn't it? Oh I'll say 'yes'. So I waited and then eventually I said 'yes', and that was it! [laughs] Nobody else wants it. Now I've got it, I can't get rid of it!"

While these seem to be the outcomes of fairly open calls for volunteers, sometimes methods of encouraging activity involved a more targeted recruitment process. From the 'recruiter's' perspective, Bob was 'pulled' and 'arm-twisted' into the organisation:

Sandra: "Frank just went up to him – he said to me 'I'm sure he'd be OK as treasurer' and he'd only been twice hadn't he? And Terry had been trying to get rid of the treasurer's job for two years."

Margaret: "You twisted his arm Frank!"

Frank: "We were desperate. And I suppose somebody needs to have a bit of background.... I don't think I knew about Bob's background then, I think he worked for himself.... Well anyway the meeting had finished and everybody had gone home and I thought 'Oh no what am I going to do now?' So I went up to him and said 'I want a word with you'.... So I asked him and he said he'd think about it, and then he decided 'yes'.... I think he did say that he had got something from the meeting. I think he said we were.... Oh I can't think of the phrase he used ... 'caring' or words to that effect – I can't remember what he said. But he thought it was worthwhile preventing it going under or something like that.... He accepted it but it was not through his own pushing."

This perspective was closely mirrored in Bob's recollection of how he became treasurer, after only having attended one open meeting.

"Anyway I went in there and Frank collared me and he said 'Look we need some help'. And I think the words 'we need some help' are probably a major trigger for me. I said 'What is it?' He said 'Our treasurer's got a major problem. He's been in hospital. We need somebody to take over from him. Would you be interested? He only just lives down the road from you.' I said 'OK I'll go and talk to him. Find out what it's all about. See what I can do'.... Anyway I said I'd have a go at the treasurer's job. And so effectively I didn't volunteer – I was recruited.... He collared me. He twisted my arm. 'Will you help?' I think that was the trigger for me.... Somebody was

asking for help. It was something I could do, and it didn't seem as if it would interfere too greatly with the time that I'd got available. So the combinations were right."

Bob described it in retrospect as a reciprocal meeting of needs:

"Why you get into these things is that there's a need on your side and a need on another and the two combine to form a mutually common objective.... At the time I probably had a need myself in that I'd been made redundant in '91. I'd sort of done self-employment work since then. But I've always missed being part of a group. A social group.... I suppose I needed some sort of social activity, and they were really nice people. Plus the fact that I needed to learn about the medical condition.... I found they were a useful source of information.... It depends on whether I see the thing that I'm doing as worthwhile."

As well as illuminating some of the reasons why Bob was open to the suggestion of becoming more involved, albeit with the benefit of retrospective reflection, this also illustrates some of the reasons why people might continue their involvement. In Bob's view it is a matter of a worthwhile activity which continues to meet his personal needs – to learn about the condition, to help out and to continue the engagement with people he likes.

For Sandra the reasons for her initial and continuing involvement in Health Self Help derive from a personal commitment, related to her own childhood and to her identity as a Christian:

"I was very ill as a child. And nobody thought I'd live to be 21, let alone get married and have three 6 foot sons. Now I suppose really I'm so grateful that I've got where I am, I try to pay it back.... I get something back in the fact that I'm helping. I'm putting something into society.... I'm trying to be like a Christian I suppose, and I'm putting something back in.... I try to live as the Lord wants me to, so that's my unselfish way ... I've always been a Churchgoer. I've always gone to Church. You know I do the mother's union also."

Margaret saw Sandra's involvement as reflecting something about her basic nature:

"… just helping people – it comes naturally to some people – it's in your nature. It comes natural to you doesn't it?"

'Keeping going' and 'getting out'

In this section the continuing interactions between volunteers within the organisation are described. These interactions show how individuals are 'locked in' to the activities and roles which they have been given or otherwise assumed. There is a kind of 'enforced loyalty', which Bob expressed as an indirect pressure or 'undercurrent':

"It's willing horses that get all the work if they're not careful. In the end what actually keeps you in is the recognition that they're now dependent on you … there's no applied pressure but there's obviously a sort of conscious and a social pressure that's exerted … because you're there, they just expect you to do it. So there's also a sort of very sinister sort of undercurrent that draws you and keeps you in … I can understand some people would get sucked in and would find it difficult to say 'no'."

Bob has also been party to the very same encouragement or 'pressure' being applied to others to 'keep going'. Here he describes his own response to the request by the minutes secretary to relinquish her role:

"And we kept her going for quite a long time. I did it by sort of positively stroking her and saying 'Well if you look at that minutes book it's like a story … if you look back – you're the storyteller for the organisation. And *you* know what happened with this and what happened then. And the fact that you've written this in the book means that you can probably remember things that other people can't….' I think after about 17 years of doing it, why she got started doing it in the first place is probably a mystery. She

was probably recruited…. The next thing you know it's 'Wait a minute, it's become a regular routine' and so you're doing it and you're on the treadmill and … 'How do I get off?' And she kept saying 'I want to get off, I want to get off'. But you see it took two years for them to listen. And then she came to the conclusion and said 'Well look I cannot cope with this any longer. I just cannot do it'."

From this it would seem that in general terms stopping voluntary activity is a matter of negotiation, and is somewhat harder to achieve than volunteering in the first place. The barriers to exit could range from subtle encouragement and positive feedback to 'keep you soldiering on', to more direct forms of pressure and even emotional blackmail. Thus Sandra refers to the implicit contract she has made with her colleagues, and more importantly with herself, regarding her involvement:

"It's a commitment, possibly more so than an obligation. It's possibly an obligation when it was a week like last week and you're getting fed up, but I would say possibly it's a commitment. If you take something on you've got to see it through. Either before you take it on, think about the ins and outs…. I think it's really commitment. You realise that if you don't do it you're letting people down. You probably go to bed at night thinking 'Right that's it, I'm packing up'. But next morning you think 'Oh I feel a bit better' and you go on. You just keep on going."

For Sandra this is an open-ended commitment, for which some form of self-defined permission is required for its termination. The only valid reason for no longer being involved is that you cannot physically continue due to some concrete factor, such as moving away, or declining health:

"Whilst ever I can do it, I haven't got a feasible excuse for packing it in. If I was ill like Margaret was last year. If you're ill you can't, but while ever I can get to the meetings, mother's union or whatever, I haven't got a feasible excuse to pack it in. There'll be somebody else worse than me probably doing something else … you just keep on, keep on going … until … you can't do it anymore because you're ill…. I haven't got that far. I mean let's face it – I was 69 last week so I was just a youngster. When I think I can't do it and I'm not doing it right, and it really does get hard. Well then I think as I say ... but otherwise you're letting them down and it's a commitment and you keep on going."

And so back to Bob. He wants to leave, and does not appear to have some of the internal constraints of duty and permission mentioned by Sandra. For him personal needs and goals seem to be more significant factors than any notion of indefinite commitment:

"What I've been conscious of was that I never intended to take it on long term when I first joined them, and they've been in it 15, 17, 19 years and I thought I don't want that continuity. That's not what I'm looking for. I'll help them over a hurdle and out of a spot.... There is that thing that once you're in it, you're in it for life. For life? No, I never joined it for life. I joined it in terms of saying I'll support it while ever I'm able to, but as soon as I feel that I can't give it the 100% commitment that I want to give it, then I shall have to leave."

For Bob, changed circumstances, and the need to concentrate on building up his business, mean that he can no longer give that degree of commitment. Bob has also found that the role of treasurer has increasingly become a burden. It's a chore – something which he doesn't feel particularly connected to, in contrast to the areas of work in Health Self Help he had found enjoyable: being an unofficial 'information officer' or as an expert on some of the latest news and developments in this area. In terms of wanting to negotiate an exit from Health Self Help, Bob is clear that the work he is doing is no longer fulfilling the needs it once did.

However, the power of the undercurrent, of 'enforced loyalty' and of not wanting to let people down, is still apparent. It may not be fulfilling Bob's needs, and may not be so enjoyable any more, but when presenting the news to the committee, Bob referred only to his changed circumstances.

As a coda to this tale, Bob thought that the silence in the committee when he presented the news

was evidence that they simply did not know how to deal with the situation:

"It's not sunk in. Frank has taken it on board. But I don't think the rest of them have. Because the only time they really take it on board is if you say 'Right, I'm not coming through the door again'."

As a result of this Bob thought he would have to have a more serious chat about it with Frank:

"And say: 'It's not that I want to opt out of it. It's just that I can't do it anymore'."

Conclusions and policy implications

Volunteering is a complex matter. From what we have seen in this case study it may not even be very 'voluntary' in many situations. The contingencies of how people become involved in voluntary groups, and stay involved or leave, are likely to be different in different circumstances and for different people. Volunteers are not all the same, and the immediate social context or milieu will also be different. Recognition of this suggests a number of recommendations.

The first is clearly the need for sensitive volunteer recruitment and management. In this example 'active recruitment' of volunteers seems to work more effectively in filling positions of responsibility than more passive generalised calls for volunteers. However, recruiters need to be attuned to the subtleties of encouragement and the different things which people value and which motivate them. Otherwise arm-twisting, however gently it is done, may lead either to a sense of entrapment, or to the self-defeating outcome of rapid volunteer turnover. Individuals may be flattered to be asked to do something, but there is a need for openness in terms of allowing people to say 'no' at the outset.

Linked to this is the importance of transparency about what volunteers are being asked to volunteer for. Some of the detail and extent of the tasks could be drawn up in job descriptions and the likely time commitment indicated. Such transparency has the potential additional benefit that people associated with the group or organisation are more aware of the different contributions made by particular individuals.

Some form of 'volunteer audit' (commonly referred to also as a 'skills audit') may be one way of trying to achieve a better match between activities and responsibilities on the one hand, and different motivations, skills, aspirations, time and commitments of volunteers on the other. Such a process would go some way to answering the question of whether the right people are doing the right jobs. Clearly Bob now finds being the treasurer a burden, but are there alternative possibilities for him given his skills, likes and constraints? For the less appealing tasks, organisations may need to develop task sharing or rotation, or time-limited responsibilities. Conducting an audit is not an 'off the peg' process, because the circumstances will obviously be different in different organisations.

A crucial test of the rhetorical question 'how voluntary is voluntary?' is the ability to exit or withdraw from a commitment. This can be a difficult process of negotiation. Volunteer coordinators need to be sensitive to the changing circumstances and aspirations of individual volunteers. This is a fundamental challenge, because it involves balancing the needs of the organisation to provide a service, or maybe to fulfil a contract, with the shifting needs of the individuals involved.

Governments and funders also need to recognise and remember the complexity of motivations and interactions that are part and parcel of voluntary activity. Funding to facilitate what might be called the 'organisational reflexivity' or audit suggested above could be incorporated within existing funding packages such as local authority grant aid, Single Regeneration Budgets and the work of the National Lottery Charities Board.

4

Social entrepreneurs

The social entrepreneur's role is not all that wonderful

Gwen is always being praised for the work she does. She's been at it now for a number of years; so much so that the project, 'Safety Works', is fundamentally identified as her project. She set it up, she pulls in the funding for it, and she was doing all the administration, the publicity and the management. Partly because the funding is not very secure, she is also responsible for trying to think of new innovative ways of keeping the project going.

But Gwen has had enough. It had got to the stage where she felt that she couldn't cope anymore. She'd taken some work home last night, and then hadn't done as much of it as she'd liked. It seemed to be a recurring pattern lately. She'd wake up in the middle of the night thinking of all the different things she needed to do. So she'd come in early this morning to try to finish it. And then the rest of the day, with its demands and its pressures, began to hit home. More meetings, new developments, more problems to sort out, new possibilities to consider. It was all falling on her shoulders:

"I was getting here earlier and earlier and I was taking work home at night. And I thought 'Hang on.' I was beginning to think 'no way', and doing half a job or panicking because of doing half a job. And I was sort of getting agitated and I wasn't sleeping. I kept waking up in the night and thinking I must do this and this and this."

"I can't do it. I haven't had time to do it.... Things aren't getting done. Unless I get some help we're going to go under. We're struggling to continue doing the ordinary work, and we're only then standing still."

The committee was a little shocked, although Adrian, the chair, had seen it coming. They didn't say much other than "What can we do?" – a concern from people who are generally supportive but don't really know how to change things. For Gwen this had become too much:

"It's all right to think 'Oh yes I'm Safety Works'. But it's not all that wonderful, that, is it?"

Introducing the theme: social entrepreneurs

Social entrepreneurship is a contender for the 'latest big thing' or idea whose time has come. It is seen as a new way of operating and a new style of management and leadership within (primarily voluntary sector) organisations which combines the social concerns of the voluntary sector with the entrepreneurial drive, innovation and creativity associated with the best of the private sector. It is ultimately entrepreneurship driven by social objectives. For some policy advisors social entrepreneurship is seen as a way of resolving some of the dilemmas of the postwar welfare state: of how to provide increased and improved services on limited or declining resources.

The key defining feature of a social entrepreneur is the ability to act as a catalyst by pulling together diverse 'partners' (within, and beyond, voluntary, public and private organisations) to 'invest' (money, resources in kind, time and expertise) so as to find innovative solutions to social problems. Social entrepreneurs are creative and skilful, and typically move from project to project building new alliances and developing new initiatives. Many in the voluntary sector might feel that this is intrinsic to what the voluntary sector has always been about.

A reliance on social entrepreneurship with its focus on the flair, creativity and energy of individuals divorced from their organisational and wider environmental context, gives rise to a number of potential difficulties. First it can create problems of accountability, where creative entrepreneurs act decisively and grasp available opportunities and in so doing may overlook the legitimate voices of other stakeholders. Second it is not always clear that the focus on individuals represents a reliable explanation of the (successful or otherwise) operation of a particular project. For example, if a social entrepreneur appears to fail to catalyse a project, it is not ultimately clear whether this is because they failed as a social entrepreneur, or whether it could be for a variety of other organisational and institutional reasons. The attention given to social entrepreneurship might therefore concentrate on individual factors rather than the significance of an institutional context. Finally, overloaded expectations and demands can result from an agenda which so clearly focuses on individuals. If this is the case, what then happens when people who might be labelled as putative social entrepreneurs, who are expected to weave their magic spells, simply cannot cope anymore?

Introducing the agency: 'Safety Works'

'Safety Works' repairs and recycles nursery and safety equipment, which is then distributed via health visitors to low-income families. It originated in the mid-1980s under a local Council for Voluntary Service (CVS) and was funded through the Manpower Services Commission. It became independent in 1990, moved to its own premises and then became a registered charity in 1993. Of the staff, Gwen, the 0.8 full-time equivalent (FTE) project manager provides the

organisational core of the organisation. She was originally a CVS employee and was instrumental in establishing Safety Works, first as an ongoing project and then as a separate organisation. Now it has four paid staff (3.4 FTE, which has increased from 1.8 FTE a year ago), who are split between the workshop (2 FTE workers) and the office (1.4 FTE workers), where all the administration, requests for equipment and project management takes place. This small office, in the corner of what has become a fairly hectic and cramped building, also has to double up as a temporary overflow space for stored equipment awaiting collection. In addition to paid staff, Safety Works has five regular volunteers and usually takes three New Deal placements in the workshop. Safety Works had an income of nearly £40,000 in 1997/98, made up from a number of three-year project-related funding regimes, although its income continues to grow through further successful funding applications.

Safety Works is managed by a committee of seven members, which meets on a monthly basis in an upstairs room. A chairperson and treasurer are elected at the AGM each year, although it is sometimes very difficult getting and keeping hold of a treasurer. Four members of the committee are health professionals working in local communities. These provide a close link to service users, but more direct attempts to encourage users to come onto the management committee have so far been unsuccessful.

Social entrepreneurs: what's in a name?

Adrian, the chairperson, is a bit sceptical about the idea of 'social entrepreneurship':

> "I think I have difficulties with the concept as it conjures up these Branson type characters ... and I think it's quite a romantic notion."

But for some people Gwen would be a clear example of a social entrepreneur. She has developed a particular project which has now successfully expanded, become an independent charity and operates out of its own premises. She has done this by taking particular opportunities as they have arisen (for premises, equipment and raw materials and for volunteers) and by developing innovative ideas. It seems to be part and parcel of what she does to ensure that her project continues. At the moment she and colleagues in other organisations are putting a proposal together to take over and refurbish a building, allowing Safety Works the opportunity to expand from its currently cramped premises. There are few similar projects in the country, let alone the district, and the demand for the service remains as strong as ever. However, she does not particularly accept the label 'social entrepreneur'. Gwen associates entrepreneurs with much bigger things:

> "I see us as being enterprising, which to me is thinking up new ideas new ways of doing things to survive and to deliver your service. I suppose other people could see it as being entrepreneurial really but I feel we're not big enough to see ourselves as being entrepreneurial. I prefer community enterprise. That's a more comfortable phrase. I see that as communities helping themselves or helping each other to support each other within those communities. But at the same time realising that you do have to survive and maybe you do have to be a bit of an entrepreneur to do that...."

How does this 'enterprise-for-survival' work in practice? One example over the last two years has been continued thoughts around Safety Works becoming a fully-fledged 'community enterprise', whereby the workshop would be used to make products for sale so that an independent income could support the core work. Eventually this idea was partly shelved because it was felt that Safety Works would be taking on a series of large risks which might then distract it from its core task of providing safety equipment for low-income families.

For Safety Works several issues come out of the discussion on social entrepreneurs. It is not a language that they can readily acknowledge and adopt. The associations it conjures up are too near to big business. However, acting in an 'enterprising' way is more acceptable. Even so, 'enterprise' is only considered as a term or label if it is seen as a solution to the perennial concerns of insecure and inadequate funding.

> "I think we're enterprising, because we have to be."

The unbearable burdens of being a social entrepreneur

Social entrepreneurs are expected to work wonders within organisations, but this may have its limits. In Safety Works' case it was the continuing shoestring nature of the operation which led to Gwen's desperate plea for help. Overall responsibility for running the service, for taking requests for equipment, for developing new funding proposals and innovative ideas such as the 'community enterprise' arm all rested with Gwen. As the project has grown in terms of what it does, her role has become more complex, and more demanding. Meanwhile the core administrative and management of Safety Works has not grown in turn.

> "You know it was beginning to make me not very well. So I've said *you've* got to do this otherwise I'm going to go."
> (Gwen)

[The *'they'* in question are the members of the management committee of Safety Works, who, from Gwen's position, had been a constant source of frustration.]

> "They sort of said 'Well what can we do?' And I thought 'Well *you* think what you can do'. I said 'We must have some admin support. That's really what I need. We need it to make the project flow properly, to provide the service and to make sure all the other things are done. Like the finance, and the applications.... I just don't have time to do it. I'm just not getting it done...'."

Adrian sums up the overall position as he saw it:

> "If Gwen wanted to leave, I couldn't honestly say at the moment the management committee would be strong enough or active enough to take that on. It would have to. We'd have to recruit someone else ... whatever. But it's almost like the management committee has come after Gwen as it were, rather than before and that's the weakness of Safety Works – that it's quite tenuous in terms of its organisation. So I have to be pessimistic about the extent to which the management committee collectively is able to ease the burden off Gwen.... As

an organisation it does have a weak committee. That does present obstacles in terms of its future development."

A light at the end of the tunnel?

Gwen's stresses have eased somewhat since the ultimatum, because shortly after her plea to the committee, an earlier funding bid was successful. Gwen was then in a position to employ somebody because for once the bid allowed for some dedicated administrative time. This has enabled Gwen to concentrate on more managerial responsibilities such as finance, volunteer training and staff supervision, as well as her developmental role.

The developmental side of the work includes what might be seen as the more entrepreneurial elements. For Safety Works this includes involvement in a partnership with other organisations that have a semi-environmental character, which would involve a possible move to larger premises. Gwen has been struggling to keep up with all the developments around leasing and the refurbishment of a community building, and has only been able to do so because of a close working relationship with a development worker from one of the other partnership organisations. If the plan is successful, it would enable Safety Works to expand its service to meet increasing demands for equipment, take on more New Deal trainees and expand the training aspects of its work, and also begin to develop a modest commercial arm involving the sale of workshop products. A development worker would have the task of promoting Safety Works' core service as well as promoting the small range of goods it can produce in the workshop.

For Gwen there is a strong link between the ability to carry out this work and remain on top of what is going on, and the daily frustrations back in the office. Having an administrative assistant has:

"… given me time to get a bit more involved with the partnership, because previously I couldn't spare the time. And we are still making things and selling things. We're looking at ideas because we want to put a small catalogue together which we can distribute about the goods that we make ourselves. I feel much

happier about negotiations about a new building because I feel as though I've got the time to do it now, whereas before,… well I knew we would have to move but I didn't know how we were going to do it."

Social entrepreneurs need to be freed from ordinary organisational constraints to be able to be enterprising. It cannot simply be assumed that 'being enterprising' is something that a project worker or manager either can or cannot do. The existing organisational context is crucial in this regard. Thinking of moving to larger premises, and of developing a small commercial facility to support the core work seems to be possible only when that core already has sufficient capacity (at least in terms of administrative input).

The future is bright

One danger of the idea of social entrepreneurship is that projects become seen purely as the products of gifted and creative individuals. Gwen expresses her concerns via everyday examples:

"I mean just going on a week's holiday. And I would think 'I don't want to go on holiday because I can't bear to think what's going to meet me when I get back.' Now it's fine. I can do that."

Now that two extra members of staff are involved, she feels a little more confident about this:

"Well people used to say that 'Safety Works is you' and I used to find that very daunting. I used to think 'Oh dear'. But now I can say to them 'No, Safety Works is all of us.' And we all have our roles to play, and we've been able to sort of whack out the roles if you like, and review them. On a six-monthly basis we will review them. So it isn't me … in other words if I went under a bus tomorrow it would carry on. Because somebody knows what happens in here now. Whereas they didn't before. It feels more bedded down, and probably because of that I would feel a lot more happy leaving it."

Within organisations there is also the need for some re-education about roles and the apparent indispensability of key workers. Gwen spoke of trying to reassure her long-standing workshop supervisor that he need not 'chain her to the office desk', that Safety Works could continue if she left. In actual fact, Safety Works will be in this position in the medium term, as Gwen is now approaching her retirement:

> "I'm 57 this year so come three years time I'm off! No hanging around! So I want to leave this in a position that they can just pick it up. Really in the last six months I need to become almost surplus to requirements. So these are long-term things but you have to start thinking now because time goes so quickly."

This will involve the recruitment of a successor, and both Gwen and Adrian separately expressed doubts about the possibilities of doing this smoothly. Gwen thought the management committee hadn't really given much thought to her forthcoming retirement, whereas Adrian was doubtful that the wide variety of skills which Gwen has developed would be available at typical voluntary sector salaries. The current emphasis on the skills of social entrepreneurs may need to be complemented by attention to the levels of pay for voluntary sector workers.

> "Gwen has built up the project over the last few years and as with any small project it has been reliant on one person. I dread her going actually, but realise that at some stage we're going to have to start planning for that. And part of the problem is that the nature of the role is so all embracing. So many different skills, that I know it can be difficult to recruit people for that sort of project." (Adrian, Chair of Safety Works)

It might be quite hard to marry the notions of entrepreneurship and voluntary sector as conventionally understood. This difficulty often comes in a practical guise, in that finding and paying for the skills of a social entrepreneur might stretch the resources of a lot of voluntary organisations. Similarly the organisational context for a putative social entrepreneur may militate against 'enterprising' activity.

Adrian's concluding thoughts are, ironically, less opposed to contemporary descriptions of social entrepreneurs than he realised:

> "Entrepreneurship is a way of imposing a sort of small business mentality upon the voluntary sector. I wouldn't use the word entrepreneurs. I would say we are catalysts."

Conclusions and policy implications

Both Gwen and Adrian are in some ways sceptical about the language of entrepreneurship. Instead they seem to be more at home with conventional voluntary sector characteristics described in terms such as innovation, creativity and flexibility. Whatever terms are used, it is clear that current policy enthusiasms (whether New Labour's enthusiasm for 'Compacts' between local authorities and the voluntary sector, Education and Health Action Zones, Millennium Volunteers, or New Deal Programmes) threaten the fragile shoulders of voluntary sector social entrepreneurs.

Policy makers therefore need to recognise the limits on the role of project managers or social entrepreneurs. It is likely that they will be the focal point of different expectations from a number of different sources: from funders, trustees, local officials, service users and other staff members. Unless more realistic expectations can be developed, overload may result. This is particularly so when social entrepreneurs, almost by definition, are supposed to create more of an impact from fixed or reduced resources, and it will be important to address the financial context in which they operate. It seems that the overall funding regime which Safety Works experiences means that it is continually in the business of seeking to juggle time-limited funding and replace it with more secure forms of core funding.

There is an equal need for voluntary organisations themselves to consider closely the dynamics of their internal relationships. In Safety Works' case, Gwen's initial reluctance to speak out about her unmanageable workload compounded a situation where management committee members and others were apparently content to leave her to deal with the multifaceted and demanding aspects of running an increasingly complex organisation. Thus a situation often develops where key decisions are being made by individuals without much in the way of support from committees. It is clear that organisational and committee training could benefit from addressing these issues in an attempt to clarify boundaries and lines of accountability.

A further organisational constraint relates to the skills and experiences which can be drawn on within and beyond individual organisations in order to support ongoing work and develop creative ideas. It is unlikely in the near future that the burden that is often placed on individuals within the voluntary sector is going to diminish, and so it is necessary to think of ways of developing support structures for those individuals. This could occur within organisations, in terms of training strategies to develop the skills of colleagues, but could equally occur between organisations, in terms of informal peer supervision or mentoring. At best this only happens on a fragmented and ad hoc basis at the moment. Interorganisational learning is a relatively untapped area of support for individual workers and organisations, and perhaps exchanging information about how similarly placed individuals dealt with particular challenges and issues could provide an important source of support for social entrepreneurs.

5

Stakeholders and issues of accountability

Service users were not consulted

"The contract was put out to tender and we lost it. That was a very lengthy, difficult, unhappy period – particularly for our service users, who were left with such uncertainty about the future and about the service they would receive. They were not consulted during the tendering process, and were very unhappy about it. Lots submitted formal complaints but the decision still went ahead. We tried to get the local authority to meet users to explain their decision – that did not happen. We have now handed over the service, with huge sadness." (Manager, Kids–Care)

Disempowerment

"If I was to use one word to describe the impact on workers, users and volunteers of all the changes which have taken place since the project was first set up, it would be disempowerment. It sums it up really that you are having to talk to us, rather than being able to talk to our service users or carers." (Project worker, Kids–Care)

Introducing the theme: stakeholders and accountability

What exactly is a 'stakeholder'? In general terms it is anyone with a relevant interest or concern. In relation to an organisation, it is more helpful to think of stakeholders as being "any group or individual who can affect, or is affected by, the achievement of an organisation's purpose" (Winstanley, cited by Hart et al, 1997, p 190). There is some sense from these general definitions that stakeholders might have a legal or ownership interest, or be a beneficiary or investor – a categorisation which can be interpreted to be equally relevant to a voluntary agency. Although they may share some level of commitment to its aims and objectives, different types of stakeholder will experience an organisation in different ways, and will have different perceptions and expectations of it. There may even be conflict between the expectations and objectives of different stakeholders – between paid workers and volunteers, for example, or between funders and service users. Furthermore, different stakeholders will exert varying degrees of control and influence over an organisation, either at a strategic level, an operational level or both.

To be sustainable, an organisation must reconcile the sometimes divergent interests of its stakeholders, but specific outcomes will reflect the different levels and spheres of influence which they have – whether that influence is:

- either conferred by the organisation's internal ethos and values, or by external legislative frameworks;
- or commanded by the resource contributed by the stakeholder, the organisation's reliance on it and any contractual relationships which exist.

It is clear then that the activities and dynamics of individual voluntary organisations will reflect the interests and influence of a range of different stakeholders, who might variously include users, funders, paid workers, management committee members or other volunteers, and the wider community. A particular feature of the last decade has been the increased salience of accountability to stakeholders, particularly internal accountability to users and external accountability to funders. This chapter explores the differential depth and dynamics of accountability in one organisation. It will also demonstrate that the status and role of different groups of stakeholders are not immutable; that the boundaries of their spheres of influence shift over time in response to changes within the voluntary organisation and in the wider policy and financial environments in which it operates.

As in other chapters in this report, there is an inevitable overlap with some of the themes discussed in more detail elsewhere. The narrative here will thus also illustrate the impact of the external statutory agenda, and the contradictions between that agenda and the values and identity of the organisation concerned, while focusing on the implications for internal stakeholders, particularly service users and volunteers.

Introducing the agency: 'Kids–Care'

'Kids-Care' is a project based in a county town in the South West of England, but serves a wider catchment area, providing support for families who have a child or young person with physical disabilities and/or learning difficulties. Kids-Care promotes partnerships between children, parents and the volunteer carers with whom the families are individually linked to enable children to remain in their own families and communities. In addition the project aims to speak out on issues of social policy affecting children with disabilities and their families, to raise awareness of their needs in order to encourage positive attitudes and increased and improved service provision in all sectors.

Kids-Care began as a small, locally based, independent agency in the early 1980s with just two workers, a three-year funding commitment from two charitable trusts, and a management committee largely made up of its founder members – 10 parents and 10 volunteers. At the

end of the trust funding, social services were approached but at that time were not interested in supporting the project. After local negotiations with the regional director of a national charity seeking new areas of work, the project was incorporated under its wing and financed through the charity's own charitable funding, seemingly indefinitely. However, there have been dramatic changes in the fortunes of the project since that time. These have been the result of changes in the policy, financial and organisational environments in which it works rather than any changes in the needs and wishes of service users – those stakeholders who prompted the initial foundation of Kids-Care.

In the last seven years the project's care support service has experienced:

- a shift from being financed through charitable funds to being entirely funded through a social services' contract;
- a resultant partial marriage of the project's care support service with social services' own provision, with very different procedures and mechanisms for relating to users and volunteers;
- the subsequent loss of this contract and the handing over of Kids-Care families and volunteer carers to another provider, after the service was put out to tender.

The chapter will illustrate the influence of different stakeholders on the project, and the impact of the above changes on the balance between internal and external accountability. The data quoted is derived from separate interviews with two project workers and their line manager within the charity. It was not possible to interview service users or volunteers, however, because of:

- a concern that this would overlap with research the charity itself was undertaking to evaluate exit strategies, and
- anxieties at management level in relation to the sensitivity of the issues to be covered, given the agency's concern not to jeopardise their continuing relationship with statutory funders on other areas of work.

Ownership and the role of stakeholders

The first watershed in terms of the role of its original stakeholders – the parents – was when the project was taken on board by a national charity. The existing management committee, which consisted largely of parents and volunteers, became an advisory group which related to the management hierarchy within the wider charity through the paid project leader. Although the charity now clearly managed the project, and the parents and volunteers accepted the fact that "this was the price they would have to pay for secure funding", nevertheless the Kids-Care advisory group initially remained an important body – consulted and reported to by the paid workers.

Over time, however, the advisory group has become moribund and some of the reasons for this relate to changes in the wider organisation. Because of declining charitable income and the resultant financial constraints within the national charity, an internal review of its strategic objectives moved the focus away from direct service provision towards more developmental work in the areas of advocacy, participation and communication – to ensure that its work was focused in ways which have the widest possible impact. In line with this change in emphasis, individual projects such as Kids-Care have also diversified. Furthermore its new activities are not limited to the local area. As the care support service became relatively less significant within the project, the advisory group lost touch with, and became less relevant to, the project's wider aims and objectives.

Later, the contract negotiated with social services in 1992, and the resultant service specification, left little room for the advisory group to play any meaningful role, and users simply lost interest in being involved in it.

> "We don't have a functioning advisory group and haven't done for some years. It still exists in name – but with only two current members. There have been attempts to recruit new members in the past, but there's been no interest. I think the reduction in influence they had on decisions led to them feeling that they weren't actually performing a very useful role.

> "Once we went into a contractual arrangement when so many things were ... you know when it wasn't possible to change things ... they didn't have any influence on our practice any more. At one time for example, if we were developing a new form, we would consult parents and volunteers about it and make sure it was user friendly, but once we were in a contractual relationship with the local authority – *we* [the paid workers] had no say over the content of forms, let alone the parents and volunteers. There were less and less things we could consult them on. They lost their role I suppose really.

> "I think another issue is the changing direction of the service. When you're talking about stakeholders, a number of members of staff – myself included – were no longer working on family links. We felt the advisory group wasn't as relevant to the other developments which staff had responsibility for. We did consider having different advisory groups for different areas of work. This might have worked better but we didn't do it in the end.

> "In addition, other developments in the project in recent years have not been based locally, so really their role in contributing – or even being knowledgeable about those other aspects – has been limited. The project has gone from being care support, to this being only one fifth of what the work is about.

> "A lot of members of the advisory group were puzzled by the direction the project had gone in; they didn't understand what we were doing, and they weren't necessarily that interested in some areas of the work because it didn't directly affect them. I certainly know one or two who resigned who said to me 'Well I don't really feel I understand what's going on any more' – and I can understand why they didn't. Meetings were just a reporting of what we were doing. It wasn't that meaningful to them. We lost that knack of making things meaningful." (Project worker)

The contract culture, organisational autonomy and the role of stakeholders

The reliance on statutory funding is a key element in the analysis of the role and influence of different stakeholders in this agency. It is important therefore to understand the internal context for this shift in funding. As a result of increasing internal financial constraints, the national organisation had decided in the early 1990s that it would not continue to fund from charitable income what were now seen as statutory areas of work following the implementation of the Children Act. It became necessary therefore for the Kids-Care line manager to negotiate a contract with social services if it were to be able to continue its work. Initially Kids-Care continued to be partially funded through the national charity, but within a few years the service became entirely funded through statutory contracts. As the principal financial stakeholder, social services were able to effect key changes in the ways in which the service was delivered. This often took place without consultation with users and carers, and despite the project's explicit objective:

> "… to encourage the wider participation of children in the development of the project by creating greater opportunities for them to speak out on issues affecting them. This will include greater emphasis upon choice for children in the way services are provided."

In effect the contract imposed on Kids-Care the processes used by social services, based on a model which involved very different procedures and mechanisms for relating to service users and volunteers.

> "Once we were in the contract, we discovered that our role was no longer to work with the family and make the link with a volunteer. Local authority social workers would work with the families and our role was in recruiting, training and approving volunteers and to support them in providing the service. In theory there was a clear dividing line. In practice it did depend on the individual social worker – because there was no doubt that the process worked better if there was one worker looking after both sides. So some social workers would allow us to

> work as we had always done; others simply wanted to use Kids-Care as a resource." (Project worker)

The changing balance between internal and external accountability

A more stark example of the difficulty experienced by voluntary sector agencies in reconciling the expectations of different stakeholders arose towards the end of its first three-year contract with social services, when Kids-Care found its future caught up in a wider strategic debate within social services. A number of outcomes were possible as a result of this internal review, one of which was that Kids-Care services might be absorbed into statutory provision. Although the future was clearly very uncertain, the workers were not permitted to discuss the situation – far less consult – with service users. As a result they felt both professionally and personally compromised.

> "I had to go into advisory group meetings with users, knowing I had been gagged. This would have been unimaginable in the past – in a project driven by users. However, throughout our first contract, social services tried consistently to get us to do away with the advisory group. This came up at every steering group meeting – that it was no longer necessary. I felt social services wanted us to be accountable to them – not to see users as the constituency to which we were accountable. However, we must retain that if we are to keep the ethos of the service." (Project manager)

Complex stakeholder agendas

As discussed in the introduction to this chapter, the sustainability of an organisation depends on the extent to which it can balance and resolve the sometimes divergent interests and concerns of different groups of stakeholders. Where there is conflict between stakeholders, it may also depend on its ability to represent those interests effectively, particularly the interests of its internal stakeholders. The concerns of different stakeholders, however, can change over time – their own agendas will not be fixed. It is interesting to consider, for example, the very different dynamics and outcomes on another occasion when further service changes were proposed by the local authority without consulting users. This proposal would reorganise and fragment the service, and limit the role of Kids-Care so that they would no longer have any involvement in certain key aspects of the service which would then be provided exclusively by the local authority's own in-house scheme. In addition to the very strong feeling within Kids-Care that users had a right to choose who their service was provided by, it is clear that there were other organisational concerns about its own future funding and status if the scope of their role were diminished, if Kids-Care no longer came within the same statutory regulations and staff were not involved in children's reviews.

> "What was behind this proposal politically I'm not sure – it may have been funding – but there was a feeling here that the intention was to diminish our role even more. It would then be possible for Kids-Care to be treated by the local authority in the same way as any other voluntary organisation." (Project manager)

Rather than providing a statutory service, the organisation feared it would be marginalised and vulnerable. On this occasion Kids-Care invited two senior social services managers to speak to users and carers at an open meeting. The vociferous objections expressed that evening resulted in a U-turn by the local authority.

> "We set the meeting up and worked quite hard to make people see the significance of what the local authority was proposing. We were concerned about the services users would be receiving in the future – but we were also concerned about Kids-Care as an organisation and our survival. The room was full – it was an evening meeting – and the two local authority officers were given a very hard time. If the proposal had gone through, what it would have meant for families is that they would have had a change of provider and link worker. The meeting grew very heated. It was the most heated meeting I've ever attended with users. I was surprised at the strength of feeling – people got angry and actually shouted. There was a lot of comment that people preferred getting the service from a voluntary organisation – that if they rang

social services the person who answered would not know them, that they had had dealings with social services in the past and didn't want to go down that path again. They liked Kids-Care and what they got from us, and the local authority should not be changing that. But there were also objections that there had been no consultation – that it was only through Kids-Care that they had even heard about the proposals. People were very angry that things were being 'done unto' them again." (Project worker)

In this example it is possible to observe not only a shift in the balance of influence between the stakeholders – between the funders and a coalition of service users and project workers – but also the different organisational concerns within the local authority and Kids-Care which might explain their separate behaviours. In addition to very legitimate concerns from their different perspectives about the nature of the service, each also had other less explicit interests in relation to their own internal finance and status.

A hierarchy of interests

In this case study it is possible to observe a hierarchy of interests and influence at work – a hierarchy which changed over time and in response to different issues. There was clearly a continuous tension between the influence of funders and service users, and this is also illustrated by our opening quote from the project's line manager in relation to the loss of its contract following competitive tendering. However, one group who were particularly marginalised by that process were the volunteers.

> "As a project we had a difficult decision to make about whether we tendered. It is against this organisation's policy to enter competitive tenders – we are against the notion of children's services going out to tender. We could have said 'no' but we would then have been seen as letting down our users. It placed us in a compromising position. But because we felt a deep commitment to users and were aware of their concern that we should continue to provide this service, we decided to tender. This was the 'least

worst' course of action – and it meant that the outcome was the local authority's decision not ours. In response to the tendering process, some parents wrote to the local press. Some put in formal complaints about the lack of certainty about future services for their children and the lack of consultation about the implications of the decision. But all to no avail. They presumably must have had responses from social services but, judging by the letters we have had, people were not satisfied with the answers they were getting.

"In addition when families were later notified of the change of provider, we had to remind social services that they had not written to a single volunteer. Volunteers were in fact very distressed – but have now been transferred to the new provider." (Project manager)

Conclusions and policy implications

Over the past seven years Kids-Care, and in particular its volunteers and service users, have in some senses been caught in a pincer movement between the legitimate organisational concerns and interests of the national charity (its foster parent) and the statutory sector. Partly as a response to internal financial constraints, the charity redefined its strategic objectives – first away from funding 'statutory' services and then away from direct service provision, towards more developmental work. The implications for Kids-Care were that within three years it moved from being a project funded by charitable income, to one which was entirely funded by a social services contract. Through the latter, the local authority purchaser was increasingly able to define and control Kids-Care's support service at both an operational and a strategic level, in response to its own internal constraints and organisational objectives. Like other voluntary organisations in the 'contract culture', Kids-Care has since seen its contract put out to competitive tender, subsequently losing the service it had provided since the early 1980s.

Through this case study it is possible to see:

- the interplay and interdependence of some of the different stakeholders who have an interest or concern in a voluntary organisation;

- the extent to which the interests of stakeholders may diverge and conflict with one another;
- the complex and changing internal agendas which determine their behaviour;
- the different levels of power held by different stakeholders, and the extent to which these may change over time.

In a world of increasing competition (whether implicit or explicit) for scarce resources, it is often the relationship with funders which is potentially most fragile and, depending on the voluntary organisation's reliance on it, most influential. Voluntary organisations are clearly concerned to maintain service delivery to users and, while not losing sight of their values in relation to organisational autonomy and user accountability, may nevertheless be compelled to compromise these to some extent. In this example, as the range of stakeholders grew, as strategic power was increasingly held by the statutory funder, accountability to service users and volunteers was eventually diminished.

Accountability to, and participation by, users and volunteers may be limited by wider organisational agendas which reflect the multiplicity of (sometimes conflicting) priorities and interests held by stakeholders, who in turn have unequal levels of power. Consensus between stakeholders may not always be possible. Where consensus cannot be achieved, concurrence may be compelled – either by the most powerful stakeholder or perhaps by direct action or representation by combined groups of stakeholders. It will nevertheless be important for each voluntary organisation, its funding partners and internal interest groups to map out in principle the legitimate spheres of influence over policy and practice for different groups of stakeholders, and to ensure that mechanisms exist for developing policy and practice which are not merely inclusive but are also empowering.

6

Managerialism

There is now a real tension in the organisation

"On one occasion two of my social workers needed me because they had been having problems with social services in relation to a client. They tracked me down at a managers' 'away day' and saw the plush surroundings and the wonderful lunch that had been laid on for us. Being angry and frustrated already, they shouted and were very stroppy. One or two people at the 'away day' later described this behaviour as very inappropriate. But no it wasn't. Those social workers were acting on behalf of service users at the time, they needed senior support and couldn't get it. There is now a real tension in the organisation. Whereas we all used to be working towards the same end, now some are working to dictats from the Finance and Admin Committee, and others are working for service users." (Service manager, London Ethnic Support Services)

From charitable effort to corporate organisation

"The working culture and practice of voluntary organisations has changed considerably over the past decade ... senior voluntary sector professionals have necessarily colluded in turning charitable effort into corporate organisation." (Chief executive, London Ethnic Support Services, Annual Report 1998)

Introducing the theme: managerialism

Many commentators on the voluntary sector have observed a shifting balance between 'voluntarism' and 'professionalism' and the adoption of managerialist techniques from the public and private sectors. Structures and processes within any organisation evolve, however, not only in response to changing external demands and the environment in which it operates, but also as a result of organic change and growth. This chapter describes these processes in one voluntary organisation and highlights some of the resultant tensions and ambivalences from two different perspectives – those of the organisation's chief executive of 10 years standing and a longer established second tier service manager. While the chief executive's account describes the problems and tensions in moving towards a new world of corporatisation, managerialism, cost centres, strategic planning, contract compliance and new technology as transitory, the case study will suggest that there may be more enduring conflicts between this new organisational culture and surviving 'traditional' values and approaches within the organisation. Some of these tensions are captured in the comments of the service manager and are encapsulated in the quotations above. The challenge for organisations such as this, which find themselves playing an increasingly central role in the delivery of welfare services (their working practice buffeted by changing legislation, increasing regulation and contract specifications), will be to define structures and processes which reconcile these demands with those elements of its own ethos which it values and which also continue to be relevant to its core objectives.

Introducing the agency: 'London Ethnic Support Services'

'London Ethnic Support Services' prides itself on being:

> ... one of the most professional voluntary agencies, providing the most comprehensive range of social care services, in the city. (Annual Report 1998)

Its activities include four service areas:

- *Older people's services:* a social work team provides advice; counselling; practical and financial support for clients and their carers; specialist work with people who are visually impaired; domiciliary care to 200 people every week; a day centre with 230 members; meals-on-wheels.
- *Services to people with learning disabilities:* residential care; community care; leisure activities.
- *Mental health services:* social work; supported housing; day and outreach services.
- *Work with children, families and young people:* social work; community services; residential childcare; day care; holidays.

The organisation plays a vital role in the delivery of key social care services to a community whose members have long experienced racial abuse and hostility, whose needs for many decades were not recognised by the statutory sector. It has grown in size in the last 10 years from having just 20 paid workers to now having over 120. Its turnover in 1998 was £1.2 million. The needs of the community it serves continue to grow (not least because of the demographic changes being experienced more widely in society) at a time when the agency is experiencing ever tighter financial constraints. Its statutory funding fell in 1998 and maintaining its fundraising income from within the community – which is the mainstay of its financial support – is increasingly difficult as a result of changes in the age structure of the local community and the geographic mobility of

younger, better paid professionals. Simply to maintain existing services requires a 7% annual increase in this income stream. Meanwhile three years ago the organisation negotiated a substantial contract with social services to provide domiciliary care.

Towards a changing organisational culture

The internal impetus behind the organisational changes which have taken place in recent years have been the need to create a more effective management structure for this expanded organisation; a concern to maintain and develop services to meet increased local needs in an historically marginalised community; constrained resources and the need therefore to achieve cost efficiencies.

> "We can't just keep pulling rabbits out of hats." (Chief executive)

Following a period of increasing attention to good housekeeping and (continuing) staff rationalisation, particularly at middle management level, the strategic response by this organisation has been a radical re-structuring of its management, and the introduction of formal business planning, service cost centres and project reviews.

- The executive committee and general committee have been replaced by a smaller board of management.
- Five specialist groups have been created beneath this. They are responsible for finance and administration, fundraising, public relations, development, and social care services – the last of which coordinates four subgroups which manage each of the service areas; service managers report to these four subgroups or management committees.
- Most recently, each service area now has to develop a costed development plan which is integrated into an annual corporate plan, approved by the board.

> "We now plan much more scientifically." (Chief executive)

The influence and skills of key individuals with a business background were critically important in defining and implementing these changes. The process was led by a newly elected chairman who has a business background, and by the chief executive assisted by the financial manager. At the time when she was appointed to this agency, the financial manager had been:

> "... one step away from going back to the private sector – she could not stand working in the voluntary sector any more – it was doing her head in. She could see how much more efficient the sector could be.... She has been able to help me corporatise." (Chief executive)

The implementation of these changes was described, however, as being 'tortuous'. There was resistance, for example, by some members of the management board, who said:

> "'What do we want all these daft plans for? The masses of paper you send through – this is an absolute waste of money. We could be putting it into services!' – all the sorts of things we've all said about the statutory sector! But you find yourself defending it because it is valuable in an organisation of this size."

and among paid workers:

> "One of the most painful things was getting service managers in the field to write business plans. They have been dragged kicking and screaming. The first one was so difficult – because all of my service managers have come up through the ranks and they are very service focused. But they have worked through those business plans with their management committee, worked through what the service is doing, what it wants and so on, and they don't grumble about them now because it is so valuable. By doing these plans, they guarantee their own resources. They can also flag up what they want to do." (Chief executive)

Although the history and exclusion of this minority community are central to understanding the organisation's single-minded focus on service users and the determination of its board and chief executive in driving through such fundamental changes, there have also been key contextual factors which have influenced this and other service delivery voluntary organisations. The political agendas of successive governments have identified an increased role for the voluntary sector in the delivery of a range of services and initiatives. This role, together with financial constraints in the public sector, the demand for increased accountability and the development of a new managerialism within statutory agencies, have led to the erosion of grant aid and its replacement with contracts or service level agreements. A changing role and relationship between the sectors has led to a number of fundamental changes in service delivery voluntary agencies, including:

- a growing emphasis on professionally qualified paid staff, as opposed to the more developmental role they may have played vis-à-vis paid workers and volunteers;
- the adoption by voluntary agencies of the strategies and techniques characteristic of statutory purchasers – a process of isomorphism.

Increasing regulation and concerns around contract compliance have particularly contributed to the development of a heightened concern with administrative systems and monitoring and evaluation procedures, which have again influenced organisations' management culture. This is illustrated by the chief executive of this organisation in relation to a recent crisis concerning its domiciliary care contract with social services. In 1998 a sequence of events triggered by the resignation of the domiciliary care manager led to the realisation by the chief executive that the organisation could not demonstrate that it was in fact contract compliant. Its information systems proved inadequate to the task and management records had not been maintained by the care manager.

> "When the project manager left in January 1998, I decided not to employ a new manager – I combined three managerial posts and offered the position as a job share to the managers of two other services. In February social services' contracts people were due to come in and do an inspection. I had already begun to feel that systems weren't quite right. The care coordinators and operational managers seemed to be working all the hours that God sent sucking a pencil and doing manual rotas. So we had got a consultant in. I felt that there must be a computer system that could organise the rotas etc. The consultant advised that this

would be possible, though it would be necessary to customise the package. However, he also said – 'I'm not sure you can prove you're contract compliant. I'm concerned about the thinness of your management information systems.' We looked more closely and uncovered a can of worms. Basically all the original manager had done since early in 1997 was deliver the service at the point of care. For a year the necessary records had not been kept. The care delivered was good, but it was through the good care workers we had in the field. There were no records on case worker visits. Nothing had been written in the personnel files for a year. There were no systems to say what we were doing. The report by social services was damning. The inspector couldn't believe the mess – contrary to his expectations.

"We are now contract compliant again after a hell of a lot of work. It has been one of the worst years. We were a hair's breadth from disaster. But we've had huge changes to make – the new computer system is nearly bedded in, the old guard has gone and the project has been restructured. What I have set in place now is a belt and braces job so that it can never happen again. We have set up monitoring systems that enable us to cross-check information. One way of doing this is by beefing up the computer system. We have also learnt the value of bringing in a consultant to work to the chair of a management committee, to go into a project and look at whether it is sustainable, whether the systems work, whether the project is accountable, whether it is efficient. So we have just completed that same exercise now in another project and this will happen across the organisation." (Chief executive)

It is important to note the domino effect this event has had on other areas of service and the extent of the impact of the audit culture on the concerns and processes of voluntary organisations. From a senior management perspective these internal changes are felt to be a necessary change – if not a necessary evil –

"I hear myself using all this 'management speak' – but it isn't where I come from!" (Chief executive)

– and problems can be resolved by further refinements to systems and processes.

"The organisation's structure is still evolving – I'm not satisfied with it yet. The strategic managers have to learn to be more strategic and service managers have to learn to manage. We're not 'management' enough yet!" (Chief executive)

Another perspective

While acknowledging the internal conflicts to which their introduction gave rise, the view held by the chief executive is that the new management structure and strategies described earlier had now been accepted within the organisation and had begun to be successful in helping to achieve her strategic objectives, namely:

"Maximum service to users and minimum risk to trustees."

From another vantage point within the organisation, however, the manager of one of the four service areas suggests a more complex reality. What unites their two perspectives, but also causes them to differ, is the strong shared ideology that service users' needs are paramount. While agreeing that there have been benefits in the new management structure and the process of strategic planning, the comments made by the service manager also flag up important questions in relation to managerialism and the corporatisation of voluntary agencies, and identify a number of potential problems created by a more 'business-like' ethos.

Vertical subdivisions between service areas and between core functions, together with an increasing number of horizontal layers in the management hierarchy, have given rise to a degree of fragmentation of the organisation which may help focus its management, financial planning and accountability, but can also have dis-benefits in terms of mutual support, information flows, and responsiveness to clients. Furthermore, the 'professionalisation' of the organisation (its emphasis on appointing qualified staff) has meant that some long established workers have felt devalued. It has also diminished the development role of the organisation. All its existing senior service managers are 'home grown', but this will not be the case in the future. With professionalisation have also come material rewards – salary structures and perks such as 'company cars' – which the service manager suggests undermine the organisation's credibility in the local community. Finally, the identification of paid workers with the organisation and their personal investment in it, may be eroded by the organisation's new corporate image. The following comments made by the service manager illustrate some of these points.

> "I am full time and some! But perhaps not so much 'some' as I used to be, and this has been one of the effects of the recent changes. I am more selective now about what I will do in my own time. When I started work here it was community social work which I loved, and if I was called at home I was more than happy to go out to a client. I would still do that – but I resent producing business plans in my own time and I won't do it.

> "In the past we all worked together, no matter what it was. If a client needed support and we weren't in, a secretary would make them a cup of tea. You never heard anyone say 'that's not my job', and now we hear it all the time. And it's catching. I have found myself saying it because I know I can be hauled over the coals afterwards. In the past people felt they had an investment in the organisation – now everything is much harder work. And the new structure is such that if a call comes in about someone who is distressed but they do not fall into your area of responsibility, you cannot go out and deal with it. You have to find someone in another team to deal with it and of course you are not their line manager so you have no authority to require them to do it. And this has happened! Clients and service users are very inconsiderate! I don't know why they won't fit in with the criteria we have laid down, but they won't. So if you have a 60-year-old in reception who

doesn't really belong in Older People's Services and they do not have a mental health problem and they are not a child or a family – what do you do? My reaction is to go down and see them, but this kind of responsiveness has been eroded. Because you suddenly think about all the paperwork you would have to do, and whether you have the capacity to take on this case, and you haven't got colleagues you can share it with because of the streamlining, so you look for someone else to do it. That's horrible. When we were all together, we used each other for support.

> "Also I hate to say it but if you want to attract professionally qualified people, there have to be perks and there have been remarks made about the number of new cars parked outside. I have one, though I don't feel comfortable about it. I would gladly give it back – but on the other hand I'd be barmy not to take it. There have been remarks about this within the community; people are not going to give money to an organisation that buys new cars for its staff!" (Service manager)

However, different responses to a new managerial culture will inevitably reflect not only different individual values and professional needs, but also the locations of the speakers within the organisation. In this case, for example, the areas of activity for which this particular service manager is responsible have gained least additional investment from the changes which have taken place. The 'costs' experienced have therefore not been matched by the perceived benefits. There will be a spectrum of views between this and those of the chief executive which our account cannot include. The juxtaposition of these two perspectives nevertheless helps to highlight some of the potential issues around managerialism in the voluntary sector.

Conclusions and policy implications

In this chapter we have been interested in the impacts of managerialism, and unlike some commentators we have not made premature judgements about its relevance or value in the voluntary sector. It is necessary to be mindful of the variety of the 'voluntary sector' – that here we are dealing with a 'non-statutory provider' of key welfare services. It has grown in the past 10 years from an organisation with 20 paid workers to over 120 – and has an annual turnover of £1.2 million. It remains a voluntary organisation in the sense that it is non-profit with a board of management comprising volunteer trustees elected by members of the organisation (members being anyone from the ethnic group it serves who also subscribed during the year); it continues to deploy volunteers in some service areas – befriending, bereavement counselling, the day centre; it depends significantly on donations from the local community, private sector interests, trusts and charities – and has a strong volunteer fundraising committee (as well as having recently employed a professional fundraiser). It does not occupy the same territory, however, as that part of the voluntary sector where key elements are a focus on local community development, a commitment to the development of volunteers, and a concern with 'active citizenship' or enhancing participative democracy. So when we consider the effects of managerialism on this organisation, it is within the context of whether such a shift enables the organisation to achieve its service delivery objectives and at what (non-pecuniary) cost; whether there are aspects of this particular kind of voluntary agency which have been eroded or enhanced.

This organisation's new corporate structure and the process of business planning have only been introduced relatively recently, and both respondents agree that the changes have been beneficial in terms of information systems, strategic planning, and being better able to argue for the development of new services and support of existing ones. Nevertheless, the case study raises a number of questions for this and other voluntary agencies:

- about the development of a structure in which service delivery may be disrupted by vertical demarcation lines between service areas, cost centres and loci of accountability;
- about structures in which horizontal hierarchies separate out administrative/ managerial imperatives from service delivery criteria;
- about a management culture which begins to resemble that found in the statutory sector (underpinned by those principles of 'economy, efficiency and effectiveness' which led to

compulsory competitive tendering and the contract culture) – at a time when the statutory sector in a new political culture is beginning to pursue the principle of 'best value', and is also beginning to (re)consider the development of integrated service delivery at neighbourhood level.

In particular, case study research enables us to see the ambivalences, tensions and contradictions involved in deepening managerialism, and that these take on different forms depending on the commentator's organisational location and level. In this example, two partly conflicting perspectives suggest, on the one hand, that problems are transitional and can be resolved by further improving techniques and rationalising management structures. On the other hand, it is suggested that tensions and contradictions may be more permanent – perhaps for as long as the organisation contains significant mixtures of managerial values and communal values, within its management board or trustees, and among its paid staff and volunteers.

7

Strategic planning

An away day? But we had one of those just last year

It's the end of another monthly meeting of the board of trustees, but this time there's a feeling that things are on the move again. Joan, a long-standing board member, was satisfied by the renewed progress. "Ah, I think we're becoming more business-like again!" she exclaims. Meanwhile Colin, who had been approached and then elected as the new chair about a year ago, has been gently finding his feet around the organisation: what it does and how it does it. He is only gradually finding out the background and history of the organisation. Colin suggests that perhaps they should have an away day to think more strategically about what the organisation is and what its purpose is, and then to develop some plan of action for the next few years. Joan quickly responds:

"An away day? But we've had one of those just last year, just before you became chair."

She pulls out some typed notes and gives them to Colin. He's not over impressed: while there may have been an away day, and there may have been some notes, this doesn't itself amount to a strategic plan. It looks more like a set of bullet points on a piece of paper than a coherent 'game plan'.

Joan was pleased that a sense of direction and focus seemed to be returning and that the new chair of the board was beginning to get to grips with the organisation:

"I think people have felt that things were pretty much running on from week to week.... Colin's a structure man, like I am really. I'm used to working with structures. I've an organised mind. I flounder when we just sit round a table just talking ... we're in an age of strategic planning aren't we?"

Introducing the theme: strategic planning

In recent years voluntary organisations have increasingly recognised the importance of strategic planning as a way of guiding their activities. However, this is often in response to a variety of external pressures, not least of which are the (perceived) demands of funders, and some voluntary organisations continue to view strategic planning with suspicion and scepticism, questioning the relevance of its formalised language and approach to their everyday concerns. It is seen as an uninvited import from the private sector or the increasingly managerial public sector. Furthermore, strategic planning can present a fundamental difficulty for many smaller voluntary organisations – how to overcome the paradox that developing and implementing a strategic plan requires more than just an understanding of its importance; it may also require the existence of the very structures and systems which are out of reach of such agencies. Is strategic planning appropriate or even attainable for all voluntary organisations?

In Counselling Forum's case there seems to have been some strategic outlook which has been developed in the past, but this may have recently dissipated. Joan would be able to tell Colin the more detailed story – that in recent years the organisation has endured a relatively turbulent period. This involved a number of changes in direction, from ambitious plans to fundraise and expand, followed by a period of consolidation and emergency fundraising, to the pursuit, and then effectively the abandonment, of customised consultancy and training services for new 'markets' and clients. Why have there been so many changes of direction? How can it regain its sense of direction and strategy? And more importantly, since strategic planning is not simply a one-off exercise, how can it be maintained?

Introducing the agency: 'Counselling Forum'

'Counselling Forum' is a small membership-based umbrella organisation established in 1989. A high profile local disaster in this coastal town revealed the need for a more coordinated approach to emergency planning as well as the need for a forum to organise and provide training for local counselling services and disseminate ideas around good practice. Counselling Forum now has approximately 160 members, both individuals and direct counselling organisations, who receive newsletters, access to a resource library and reduced-cost training places. The forum is a registered charity run by volunteers, who are either trustees or advisors/consultants who develop and deliver counselling training courses. It is managed overall by a board of seven trustees, but there is also a separate 'joint' committee consisting both of trustees and the advisors (currently four) which meets to plan and organise Counselling Forum's training and seminar programme.

Meetings take place on a monthly basis according to a rota whereby two board meetings are followed by a joint meeting, but this pattern of meetings has been subject to change over the years. A chair, vice chair and treasurer are elected at the AGM, but secretarial support is provided by a 0.2 FTE office administrator.

A Counselling Awareness Project (established in 1990) was also part of Counselling Forum, but it is shortly to separate and become a registered charity in its own right.

Financial situation (£)				
31 March	Income	Expenditure	Balance on year	Reserves
1996	6,846	7,254	(408)	4,079
1997	5,908	8,146	(2,238)	1,841
1998	9,230	4,198	5,032	6,153

(= deficit)

The breakdown of income and expenditure for recent years hints at some organisational turbulence. In the year ending 31 March 1998 (the latest accounts available), the main sources of income were from grants from four charitable trusts (£6,850: 74%). In the 1997/98 Annual Report, Gordon, who has since resigned as chairperson, spoke of this in these terms:

> "The setback to our finances mentioned last year, when our coordinator left before generating the income we'd hoped for, was amply compensated for by some generous special assistance from our friends at the four charitable trusts. These funds are in addition to the annual donations these trusts make to us, and we are very grateful for their help."

Strategic planning in context: 'a misunderstanding'

Colin already knew of Counselling Forum when he was recruited to be its third chair. In fact he was around when it was first established, although he was not involved at the time. However, now that he is involved, he questions what the organisation's role is, could be or should be, 10 years after it was established. Does it have a role now? Would it be missed if it folded? He described his first year as chair as being one of 'finding his feet' and a gentle questioning of Counselling Forum's role and ways of working. This has been highlighted recently by a misunderstanding between Gordon (who is now one of the four advisors after stepping down from the chair) and Colin, along with the board of trustees.

Gordon was well-known throughout his period of office for always trying to pursue and develop possible new ventures. In Joan's words:

"He's a very good 'good ideas' man and 'go out and get' is Gordon, but in an organisation you need a few more to come with you. When he gets moving he moves very quickly does Gordon!"

New projects and ideas could simultaneously increase the profile of Counselling Forum and draw in some independent income. At last year's AGM an invited speaker spoke about a groundbreaking hospital counselling project and there seemed to be the possibility of replicating it in the town. A brief discussion with other advisors resulted in Gordon setting up a meeting with the appropriate hospital staff to advance discussions about the project – who should be involved, how much it would cost, where it would be based and so on. Shortly afterwards, Counselling Forum received a letter from the hospital about the discussions which seemed to be more advanced than the trustees had realised. Colin decided to write to Gordon to find out what was going on and to ask him to keep the trustees better informed. Gordon takes up the tale:

"We sort of agreed that there was just a misunderstanding. When I wrote back I said, you know 'Can you envisage me actually committing the Forum to spending a lot of money which we haven't got without consulting the trustees!' You know! Please!"

While this could be interpreted as a clash of different styles of working (Gordon's tendency to work in an entrepreneurial style compared to the more collegial approach of Colin and the board of trustees), the misunderstanding is also an example of the sometimes problematic consequences of difficulties with strategic planning. Gordon operated in the way he might normally operate in pursuing a bright idea, but for Colin and some of the other trustees this was inappropriate.

"I think the project gave everybody the collywobbles. I'm of the mindset that here was an idea; so write a report which outlines some of the advantages and disadvantages. How do we take it forward? How do we get the funding for it etc etc?"

The project seemed a risky venture partly because it appeared to be developing rapidly, but also because it was not within a previously agreed planned context. Joan refers to this in planning terms:

"There's no plan as such now, we just go from meeting to meeting. Somebody comes in with an idea and then it's worked up and it happens. That's how it works, but there's no overall plan. For me personally the policy should be 'Are we going to go there?' 'Yes we are.' 'Let's ask somebody to go and do it.' Whereas with Gordon in the chair, he'd go out and do it and then come back and say there's a possibility of work here."

The advantages of planning, and the challenges

This misunderstanding was a recent example which suggested the dilemmas which can arise for Counselling Forum as a result of not having a clearly expressed plan. Yet most people see the advantage of working to a plan of some sorts, even if it is not fully worked up with targets, milestones and performance measures. Joan, for example is clear about the benefits of planning and of working towards short-term and long-term objectives:

"Well for me it creates a structure. You know what you're working towards. There's a security within it. You've got various aims and you need to get from here to there by a certain time. But, at the same time, part of that structure and part of that looking ahead has got to have an open element, in that if something crops up we can diversify along it ... there's got to be an openness within it...."

Something of this wider awareness of how an organisation operates strategically rather than simply in terms of what it does from day-to-day has clearly been lurking within Counselling Forum for some time. This 'organisational self-consciousness' manifests itself in Counselling Forum taking regular (and at one stage annual) opportunities to stand back from its routine activities to consider where it is now and where it might go next. But there is a fundamental paradox here. Key people within Counselling Forum seem to understand the importance of strategic planning, and through their regular away days seem to be attempting to develop the foundations of a planned operating structure which guides its activities. The language of objectives, direction and plans is never far from the surface of its discussions. But Counselling Forum seems to falter in this, and seems to be going through a repeating cycle of facilitated 'away days'. Although they might re-confirm the fundamental reasons for its existence, it seems that Counselling Forum rarely moves beyond this into developing frameworks that can guide its everyday activities.

For Colin it is a matter of failing to consolidate and develop the ideas that emerge at away days.

> "I suspect that they've actually had the 'time-out' but the report was never written up with the game plan in it. Maybe because there was no report it comes round again."

However, although there may have been no fully worked up plan from the last away day, one of the main 'action points' on the 'hit-list' has actually been implemented. The day had in fact originally been specifically designed to think through the succession to the chair of the organisation since Gordon was stepping down. The group of trustees sought to decide what sort of chair would be appropriate – somebody with a high profile, with connections, or somebody more functional who could strengthen the organisation through consolidating its work. Colin becoming chair is thus a tangible outcome of that meeting. Furthermore it is also possible that one of the reasons for the lack of further development from those ideas was that Counselling Forum was to be going through a change of 'leadership'. Thus a vacuum developed after Gordon stepped down and before Colin joined and had 'found his feet'.

Never mind planning – why exist at all?

> "I think some of our vision has got dissipated over the years. At what stage do we actually raise the profile and become, yes, a leading light again as it was 10 years ago when there was a lot of enthusiasm, when it was set up and went forward. Whether it needs rekindling – I suspect the answer is yes." (Colin)

For Gordon the spark which might bring back the sense of energy is a particular profile-raising venture, and this might partly explain his eagerness to develop the hospital project. But for Colin there was a more general point about the people involved in Counselling Forum:

> "One or two of the board have been there a fair number of years, so we're not all floundering around … there is a continuity, and that's one of its strengths, but also one of its weaknesses. If there are too many people around from the past, how do you bring about the vision of change? So maybe having a chairman coming in from the outside who had nothing to do with Counselling Forum is not a bad thing."

Elizabeth, a past member of the board, not known for beating about the bush, was perhaps a little more direct in the advice she gave to Colin when she bumped into him recently:

> "When I was voicing some of my sort of doubts and concerns, Elizabeth said 'Well maybe Colin you're right. Maybe the function of Counselling Forum has finished. It should cease'. She was very clear. 'Kill it, Colin. Kill it.'"

One of the lessons which could be drawn from this analysis is that for strategic planning to have some long-standing resonance, such that it can be sustained, there must be a clear mission behind which the organisation can cohere and which it can move towards. The practical handbooks usually have this as step one or two in any strategic planning approach. Thus for Counselling Forum some of its difficulties in maintaining a plan may be down to this overall lack of confidence about what its role could or should be.

In so far as Counselling Forum is struggling to find a purpose, it has become reactive rather than strategic in the development of its ideas, and therefore devotes its energies to responding to the latest 'bright ideas' which may swing the organisation in different directions. For Joan there is now a feeling that Counselling Forum should re-focus its efforts to developing low-cost training for ordinary volunteers in its membership organisations.

Obstacles to strategic planning

Even if the benefits of planning are clear, and the existing difficulties facing Counselling Forum are also evident, getting to a stage where an organisation can work to a plan is more problematic. The capacity to plan and think strategically is a function of the particular background and experiences individual people bring to the organisation. In practice, however, the barriers to strategic planning in Counselling Forum seemed to be more intractable, and beyond the direct control of the individuals concerned.

A lack of time was one issue, since most of Counselling Forum's work was done by busy volunteers, all of whom had other pressing commitments. A planned approach may fall by the wayside in such a situation. For example, the forthcoming 'away day' session to begin to focus on elements of strategy is not going to be a day at all; because of time pressures and other commitments it will be an extended ordinary board meeting with a restricted agenda.

A second obstacle is the particular uncertain context in which an organisation might work. Funding regimes may hinder attempts to plan, but also a lack of strategic planning may restrict an organisation's horizons in terms of fundraising to achieve its goals:

> "Maybe we're in a comfortable niche where we get our funding from a couple of organisations, and maybe don't bother trying to approach others. And maybe we don't approach others because there's no long-term aim. If we do need to exist then we need to think about what are we actually about. What are we actually going to be providing over the next four or five years. How do we go about providing it?"

Counselling Forum, like many other voluntary organisations, faces a number of key dilemmas. These cover intangible issues, such as how it can find a niche, and then flourish, so that the question of whether it needs to exist doesn't even arise. They also extend to more concrete questions such as how it can cope with the contingencies of 'events', for example a worker leaving, a funding emergency or the loss of secure premises. A further distraction for Counselling Forum is that its office space is up for sale as part of a large redevelopment programme, and so its trustees are having to scurry around trying to find new premises. Strategic planning may help provide a framework for considering and overcoming these issues, but it may also be the case that an organisation faced with such difficulties is not in a strong position to be able to introduce and adopt a strategic approach in the first place.

Conclusions and policy implications

The distinction, between introducing a strategic plan and sustaining it, is vital to understanding some of Counselling Forum's difficulties, but also has wider policy implications which we have considered in a series of bullet points.

- *Purpose and mission:* Counselling Forum's story would seem to indicate some of the travails of being less than sure about an organisation's purpose. The consequence seems to be that its approaches to strategic planning hesitate at the first hurdle. If strategic planning is to become more widespread within voluntary organisations, it must be seen as more than just a paper exercise. Training providers in the voluntary sector may therefore need to refocus training courses to deal with the later 'ongoing' stages and operational difficulties about planning rather than just the initial ones.
- *Organisational 'drive' versus organisational 'drift':* Counselling Forum's experience suggests a waning of enthusiasm from the early days when it was established. The process of attempting to introduce a planned context for an organisation's work may itself have the effect of stimulating interest and activity, but it must be recognised that this may only be temporary. If levels of 'drive' and activity within an organisation are generally beginning to dwindle, it is not clear that an organisation can easily move to a state of more planned activity. Even if it is able to move beyond this initial hurdle, the momentum created by a plan may not be so easily sustained. People do not have limitless time and resources of energy, and this needs to be recognised by funders, statutory authorities and others who might suggest that strategic planning is a panacea for voluntary organisations.

- *Contingencies, turbulence and 'events':* We have seen through Counselling Forum's experience that attempts to work to a plan can easily be frustrated by the simple 'turbulence' created by 'events'. It may be for example that a new person becomes involved who has a dynamic effect on the organisation which might disrupt (possibly helpfully) previously agreed ways of working. With Counselling Forum, the mid-contract resignation of its paid coordinator, and the temporary funding difficulties that this created, caused Counselling Forum to abandon its attempts to raise its profile and activity. No organisation can be in complete control of its destiny, and it is important to recognise the limits of planning in these circumstances.

- *Organisational context: people, funding, premises:* Even if Counselling Forum had a strategy, it would still have to come to terms with the different ways people interpret their roles and carry out or fail to carry out their expected activities. Ultimately implementing a plan becomes a means by which different people negotiate with each other regarding their roles, their ways of working, the use and development of their particular skills and the objectives they seek to fulfil. Passionate advocates of strategic planning may again have to rethink the ways in which they seek to persuade voluntary organisations of its merits in situations where the context displays different degrees of fragility.

If some of the problems described above are a familiar feature of the day-to-day life of many voluntary organisations, the prospects for strategic planning within the voluntary sector are, if not bleak, certainly circumscribed. It is not surprising that voluntary organisations often view it in sceptical terms. Joan echoes the sentiments of many working and volunteering within voluntary organisations when she considered the effect on Counselling Forum of *not* operating with a long-term strategic plan:

> "I wouldn't say it's suffered but it's not progressed."

For strategic planning, it may be necessary to develop a more modest or realistic way of working; one that favours the more low key aspects of planning. Colin hints at this in summing up Counselling Forum's present position:

> "Maybe now it is time for change ... maybe not radical change but just refocusing ... but maybe this is the wrong use of the word. It's just that we're beginning to find a sense of direction again."

Rather than the 'thick' planning associated with strategic plans, business plans and operational plans replete with inputs, outputs and milestones, organisations may merely wish to develop a 'thin' version based more on the specific challenges they face. Then voluntary organisations might gain (or regain) some sense of focus by recognising the specific ways in which they currently operate, and by feeling more confident about the work they already do. We may be in an age of strategic planning, but we need to fashion strategies which are appropriate and realistic in voluntary organisations; planning for attainable aims and objectives in uncertain environments.

8

Networking

'Button-hole' and 'ear-hole'

Mary and Siobhan (two workers from Money Advice Service) were in London for an important consultation meeting. They had travelled down especially. The government department hosting the consultation uses these types of meetings as a sounding board for relevant voluntary sector stakeholders over the latest directions in government policy. Other voluntary organisations were represented, and senior civil servants were also there. What Mary and Siobhan did when they got there seems to be pure, instrumental, advanced-level networking. They had already been briefed in advance by a friendly contact in their local area:

> "We used the contacts I'd got to try and get more information. When we went down to the consultation meeting, we had been told that the guy we needed to talk to was a civil servant called Graham Chandler."

Siobhan still had it in her notebook from that meeting, written across the top corner of the page: 'Graham Chandler: ear-hole him.'

> "Some people button-hole. We ear-hole! So when we got there we sussed out who Graham Chandler was and straight away made a beeline for him. Mary goes straight across the room – phoom! I thought 'Oh my God! What's she doing?' So we collared him there ... and it was perhaps a couple of months later when he came to see us."

It is interesting that how Mary and Siobhan got to be at the meeting in the first place was through the particular networks they were involved in:

> "Dave from 'Moving On' [a national voluntary organisation] 'phoned me up and said 'Did I want to go to ... a consultation meeting in London for this new government initiative.' I mean I was suitably peeved. He'd offered me his train ticket. I said 'I don't want your train ticket. I want my own invitation!' So I phoned through the network and we got invites to go to this meeting. I 'phoned through to [the government department] and I said 'Do I have to go through [cabinet minister]?' And that was like.... 'Cos I mean we do have a lot of contact with him. And her attitude, her whole demeanour altered.... She said 'I'll get on to it straight away and I'll ring you back.' She rang back maybe 5, 10 minutes later and said 'Please come. We will pay your fare.' It was an opportunity for them to get something from us. We've been invited to that consultation group ever since."

The result of this meeting was that Money Advice Service (for which Mary is the project manager and Siobhan a project worker) was able to submit a bid for the pilot government scheme. The bid was successful, and Money Advice Service is about to start receiving the first tranche of the £150,000 to run the project. It might be stretching it a little too far, but you could suggest that they wouldn't have got this money if it hadn't been for the networking work that they had put in.

> "God, what a tangled web." (Siobhan)

Introducing the theme: networking

Networking is increasingly seen as an important aspect of the functioning and development of voluntary organisations. This is usually (and often cynically) expressed by the phrase 'It's not what you know, it's who you know'. Alongside becoming aware of new policy developments and funding opportunities and of nurturing a higher profile through network participation, 'being well networked' can involve more mundane (but arguably no less significant) matters of knowing people who you can 'tap' for information or expertise, on the assumption that this could and would be reciprocated. So far, however, there have been very few (if any?) studies which have attempted to explore how different forms of networking operate within small case study contexts.

Introducing the agency: 'Money Advice Service'

'Money Advice Service' was established in a West Midlands town in 1976 as a local advice and campaigning organisation for a specific client group. Its profile has since grown so that it is now nationally recognised for some of its work and, as indicated above, is just about to become a local delivery agent for a key government initiative. Although its profile has grown steadily, it is only in the last four years that the organisation has actually grown dramatically in terms of income and staff. As we will see, this growth is also a detailed story of networking. While for most of its history it has operated on the basis of an annual local authority grant of less than £20,000, new projects have been added in the last few years which mean it now employs five staff and has an annual income of £89,070 (1997/98 figures). The advice service remains the core of its activities, but it now also runs a couple of more developmental, time-limited training and mentoring projects for its specific client group. These projects operate under national (Single Regeneration Budget) and European (European Social Fund) regeneration funding regimes. The following table highlights its dramatic recent growth.

Financial situation (£)				
31 March	Income	Expenditure	Balance on year	Reserves
1994	19,317	19,502	(185)	2,458
1995	20,073	19,443	630	3,088
1996	27,739	26,439	1,300	4,388
1997	61,365	60,653	712	5,100
1998	89,070	90,441	(1,371)	3,729

(= deficit)

With the main share of £153,000 (over 12 months) from the new government project to be added in the forthcoming financial year, the extraordinary growth of Money Advice Service is set to continue in the foreseeable future. The core of Money Advice Service's funding traditionally came from a local authority grant, but because this has broadly remained static over the years, it now only accounts for 25% of total income. Despite this it still remains the foundation for the separate project funding, so that the net effect was described by Mary (project manager) as a 'house of cards'.

Money Advice Service prides itself on being a 'grass-roots organisation'. It was originally established by active local members of the client group and has always retained a campaigning focus alongside its service activities. Importantly it also retains a direct management structure which ensures that it is still 'run by the client group for the client group'. Local social and campaigning groups are affiliated to Money Advice Service, and its management committee is made up solely of representatives from these groups.

Networking in context

Siobhan describes networking as simply the way people interact:

"It's about people, and about people who know people...."

Our discussions with members of staff at Money Advice Service around networking centred on different possible types of networks, distinguished not by sociological criteria but by policy/practice issues. Since Money Advice Service had recently had to endure a threatened cut to its local authority funding, one type was what might be called *emergency networking*, or how you might seek to save your project from threat. Here the organisation might attempt to marshall its resources (both internal resources and, important in this context, external resources) in order to go into 'defence mode', as Siobhan described it. For Money Advice Service this did not involve direct lobbying of local councillors, but it did involve mental head counts of potential allies, and quiet soundings about the real strength of the potential threat to their funding.

A second form of networking is called *strategic networking*, or networking for service development, where participation in particular networks might enable you to achieve what you want to achieve for your organisation. A third form of networking involves that around the core work of the organisation, in this case around the delivery of particular services. For Money Advice Service this *service delivery based networking* (or how you do what you do) includes participation in a local umbrella body as well as nationally based networks.

In addition to different types of networks it is also possible to distinguish two styles of networking by the depth or 'quality' of the network relationships; we might think of network links based on longer standing relations of trust and friendship between individuals, in contrast to more fleeting encounters. What has to be remembered, however, is that these several definitions are 'ideal types', useful only as guides into a more complex reality.

Networking as 'deep relationships'

When Siobhan and Mary were asked to describe the ways in which networking had been significant for the dramatic recent developments at Money Advice Service, both referred to a specific meeting between Mary and Denise, a key local authority manager. The subsequent relationship which these two individuals developed over the four years in which Denise worked for the local authority was in their view fundamental to Money Advice Service developing its service and becoming what it is now. Siobhan described this in networking terms:

"So much [networking] seems to be particular. A particular character, a key worker, a personality. The meeting of

two people for example.... I know Mary would say 'If you had to pinpoint one single catalyst to the development of MAS it would be Denise.' I disagree with her. I think the major catalyst for the development of MAS was not Denise, but Mary and Denise meeting. The combination of these two heads, these two individuals, these two bolshy characters who both have this vision.... So I think it was the sparking off of those two minds. And Denise had the power and position to take that forward."

It is important to stress the importance of the institutional context in which the chance encounter occurred and the personalities involved. After the first time Mary and Denise had met, Mary had heard, 'on the grapevine' (or network), that Denise had found her 'intimidating'. Mary thinks she is direct and assertive, and doesn't suffer fools gladly, but was a bit upset by this:

"So the next meeting I was a bit bristly really. I went in there thinking 'You bitch, thinking I'm intimidating'."

Subsequently the relationship between Mary and Denise became one of respect; they would occasionally go for coffee to sound off about work-related things and everyday frustrations.

Two aspects of networking are evident from this analysis. Firstly networking is a function of particular institutional contexts and roles. The basis of a developing network link is a recognition of what each party can bring to an 'exchange'. The benefits of networking could therefore usually be seen as mutual or reciprocal. For Denise, Money Advice Service and Mary could bring a close grass-roots perspective on policy development with a concrete view about how a particular service would work on the ground with real people. Mary's view expresses this succinctly:

"I'm probably one of the few people of all those involved in strategy who actually deals with real people. I think I keep people's feet on the ground because of where I'm coming from.... I get feedback from people who use the services and from the groups and I know what they want and what they don't want."

Meanwhile for Mary, working closely with Denise meant that for the first time Money Advice Service had an opportunity to be involved in policy development from the beginning rather than campaigning against it after it had been implemented. On a personal level Mary feels that her relationship with Denise gave her more confidence to continue pursuing what she believed in on behalf of her clients. The fact that her voice was listened to implied that at last she was seen as having a valued input into policy development.

The second aspect of networking which it is important not to overlook is the particular relationships that are forged, re-forged, broken and deepened every day between people who work in similar fields. Networking clearly is a function of specific relationships between individuals, and therefore cannot just be seen in terms of institutional roles.

Now that Denise has left the local authority to work in a local health trust, Mary feels that her own position within the strategy group is under some (implicit) renegotiation, leaving her to some extent out in the cold. Having been a central part of a network, she is now somewhat on the edge:

> "To some people that friendship – partnership was threatening. Now Denise has gone, it's almost as if they don't know where I fit in the scheme of things. And I also feel that to some people our friendship might have been perceived to be threatening because we're both very gobby women, and neither of us suffer fools gladly, and we're both people who are willing to take a risk. And to people who are used to crossing the t's and dotting the i's that is not the appropriate procedure.... Now you can't have that intimacy and that gossipy situation where the real truth comes out. It's really quite sad. I felt I had the fingers on the pulse much more when Denise was here than I do now."

Money Advice Service's position has changed following Denise's departure. There are still links, however, and Mary continues to participate in an important strategic arena on behalf of Money Advice Service's clients. Similarly, the friendship with Denise has not waned. They still meet up regularly, and since Denise now moves in national policy circles, she often champions

Money Advice Service as a valuable grass-roots local service provider.

Networking as 'fleeting encounters'

More distanced, fleeting encounters may sometimes entail exchanges of information and expertise, or people simply 'getting on' or trying to make connections with each other when introduced for the first time; there may be only a small chance that deeper professional and personal relationships of trust will result. Networking can of course be more instrumental than this. Hence when Mary and Siobhan 'ear-holed' their pre-selected civil servant, they had particular purposes in mind.

> "We're always networking around trying to have an influence on policy and stuff ... by being in there, by being in the frame, we would have more of a chance of influencing things than if we were on the outside. We'd been on the outside for 19 years, and you can't allow yourself to be on the outside forever. Otherwise you're always going to be marginalised."

Having got Graham Chandler to visit, they used the opportunity of the captive audience to argue the case for Money Advice Service in the delivery of appropriate services:

> "We told him 'What you're proposing to do is what we do. Why re-invent the wheel? Why not fund those of us who are doing this to get on and do it. You do your bit and pay us to do these other things. Let's work together on this and together we can deliver a good service'. And he said 'The government wants some pilot projects and there'll be money to bid for'. And we said 'Right. Notify us when we can bid!'"

What these slices of life within Money Advice Service show is that in terms of networking, it might not simply be a case of who you know, but of who you can get to know and how strategically you decide to develop and participate in network links. For Mary, gaining the money for the pilot initiative was a combination of:

> "National recognition, local work,... and just being pushy!"

The reference to being pushy is important because it reminds us that networking, especially with direct instrumental goals at hand, involves time, persistence and effort. However, even a 'fleeting encounter' can act as a crucial bridge between two relatively 'deep' networks, as suggested in the following example:

> "I could leave tomorrow, and I could leave a new worker a list of contacts. But it would take her six months or whatever to make her own networks. It very much depends on the nature of the person and what you bring. I'm from this town, I've lived here practically all my life and the reason I know there's a good bingo night on at the Pheasant is because I used to go every week with my grandparents. It's just stupid things like that. It's to do with the information that's in your head because I know this town very well.... So like I don't know anything about provision on the Cedars Estate but I knew a couple of key workers. I talked with them, they put me onto a couple of people. I've tried out one of these contacts and they've proved to be very useful and they told me about somebody else, and so you bring so much of a network with you, from your previous experience and then you develop your network in direct response to the needs that are apparent. And that's the whole ethos of Money Advice Service."

Conclusions and policy implications

All voluntary organisations have some participation in different networks of contacts and alliances, if only through the particular relations and links of the people who are involved. In the same way that relationships between individual people are continually being developed and renegotiated, networks involving voluntary agencies are constantly changing and developing.

'Well-networked' organisations,

- in terms of the density of the networks (how 'embedded' an organisation is within them, 'how many people you know'; 'how well you know them')
- and in terms of how important those networks are ('who you know'),

may fare reasonably well in terms of access to information, to funding opportunities, to influence and to a safety net of support which can be drawn on in difficult times. Poorly networked organisations may face the converse. If this is somehow inherent in the nature of networks, there is ultimately a conundrum for policy makers both in local authorities and in intermediary voluntary agencies about how to approach networks. A degree of ambivalence in policy terms results, where it is not clear whether networks should be encouraged or discouraged, or whether they might simply be left alone.

In general terms networking tends to be encouraged on the grounds that an organisation is strengthened insofar as it can draw on knowledge, information, expertise and the like from other agencies or key individuals. This 'joined-up' approach is favoured in the current emphasis on partnership working across the interface between the public, private and third sectors, as well as within each sector. Networks are a way of achieving a synergy in activity which might not have been possible otherwise.

However, if networks can be a strong means of cementing relationships between individuals working in similar policy or service fields, they can also be exclusionary. The downside of the familiarity and common understandings between network links which comes from close and regular contact is that this might lead to 'insider advantage' or preference – in developing funding opportunities, for example. Membership of a network by an organisation may be a 'positional' advantage in that the benefits which are perceived to follow diminish as the network is expanded to include others.

In Money Advice Service's case, Siobhan expressed the view not only that their 'ear-holed' civil servant had given them a discreet 'tip off' about a forthcoming policy initiative, but that this advance information had enabled Money Advice Service to begin to assemble the component parts of what subsequently became a successful bid. However, there was nothing improper or underhand about this. It is impossible to know whether Money Advice Service would have been successful if they had not known that the opportunity was going to come up; but the civil servant was telling them about an initiative which had been announced in the House. The information was in the public domain. Larger organisations such as TECs and colleges can employ staff to fundraise and seek out such information; for organisations such as Money Advice Service the process of getting information is inevitably more ad hoc. In such situations, networking becomes vital in helping to create the time and space to make bids properly as opposed to rushing them off in the last few days.

Insofar as network participation confers more tangible advantages, and begins to take on a more exclusionary character, policy makers might wish to discourage networks, or devise ways of maintaining openness. This is not to say that such intervention would be straightforward. Any policy which aimed in some sense to 'police' networks, would have to come to terms with all the potential 'side deals' and informal 'off the record' discussions between participants.

An alternative policy approach to networking might simply be to leave them alone. If networking is merely an explicit term for ordinary people with shared interests 'getting on' with each other and developing relationships, however covert, it may be that policy makers cannot reasonably expect to influence (by either facilitating or 'policing') their character. Networking just happens. It may be that attempts to facilitate networks by, for example, providing sites for information exchange or setting up discussion forums, loses the informality which is the essence of much network activity. Siobhan laughed at the sometimes clumsy attempts to create 'artificially induced' networks; in this case from a central funder aiming to bring its disparate projects together:

> "I can't find it ... [looking in notebook] ... I just want the title. Get this for a title. It's something like 'Provider Support Contact Group'!... [laughs] But all credit to them, putting us in touch and facilitating us meeting. Although they've given it a silly title, they've instituted this. But the fact that we all came together in that training centre and swapped names and addresses, an informal network developed there anyway."

If networking seems to escape a single coherent policy response, there are some aspects of the illustration portrayed here which may be important for policy makers and analysts to recognise.

Firstly participation in networks is a demanding process, involving effort, time and specific social skills in terms of talking to others and developing ongoing relationships. Importantly, networking requires a degree of 'space' away from the everyday pressures of other organisational activities. Unless this is recognised by policy makers, and funders, it will tend to remain the exclusive arena for the well resourced.

> "We don't sit there because of what we think we can get out of it, but because we want to be sure that our client group is represented. An opportunity to have a voice – that's what it's all about. I get to find things out because of being part of the strategy group. It's a pain in the backside because sometimes I feel I could be doing much more productive work. But it's back to: 'If you're not there, you don't get to find out what's happening.'"

Secondly it is essential to recognise that being involved in particular networks can be a long-term and cumulative process.

Finally, however, this does not mean that network trajectories or positions are fixed. Networks are always in a state of flux because they are based on changing relationships between individuals. Relationships may wane because individuals decide not to nurture them for whatever reason (eg other work pressures, personal preferences etc). Similarly people move on in their own careers and lives, and this will have an impact on the nature of any network links which they leave behind or retain in a different form. Networking might best be seen as the charting of a particular course (however intentionally or unintentionally) through a shifting 'landscape' made up of other individuals, organisations, strategy groups, umbrella forums and consultation panels. Where you are as an individual and as an organisation depends on the combination of changing institutional structures and what you are able to bring (resources, reputations and existing relationships) to a particular networking context.

9

External agendas

"A new funding programme suddenly appeared out of the blue from the Home Office, on January 6th. It's £7 million cash, a three-year programme and organisations can apply for up to £50,000 each year. But the applications have got to be returned by 31st January! It's madness!" (Quoting from the covering letter from the Home Office which accompanied the application form.)

"Families are the cornerstone of our society and this programme will ensure that our partners in the voluntary sector can build on their exemplary work and continue to deliver quality support...." It's just absolute madness – it's 'key' and 'core' and 'strategic' and 'diddle', but we're only giving you three weeks to think about it!

"When I came back to work from having 'flu, the forms were on my desk. They are about 25 pages long – look at them! They want strategic plans, business plans, budgets and God knows what else. They want to know our salaries and national insurance for three years, and projected funding for the next three years. They want details of 'trustees' occupations, relevant experience and training'; and they want an 'organisational chart'. I don't even know what an organisational chart is! And this is just one of the forms. And we've got three weeks to do it! And there's £7 million being thrown at this programme – where has it suddenly come from?

"There is an initial reaction by voluntary agencies – 'We need to get some of this money. What can we do?' Then people start saying 'We can't do this on our own; partnership bids would be more successful – we need to get with education'. There is a flurry of activity. This is where we go wrong in the voluntary sector. In my opinion, it would be much healthier for the whole of the voluntary sector to turn around and say 'This is totally unrealistic, this is stupid. Take it away, we don't want any of it'. Funders would then have to re-think how they do things. But you won't get that – you'll get people rushing to fill in forms and create projects." (Senior organiser, Family Friends)

Introducing the theme: external agendas

Voluntary agencies are not solitary organisational islands; they operate within a broader 'ecology' of resources, legislation, policy and organisational relationships, and aspects of the event described above will be familiar to many in the voluntary sector:

- the 'out of the blue' statutory initiative;
- the recognition by policy makers of the importance of voluntary sector 'partners' at an instrumental level, but not always at a strategic one;

- the social and financial significance of the new initiative – alongside an improbable time-scale;
- the questions posed for the voluntary agency: 'Can I/should I respond?'; 'What are the costs and consequences?'

The ability and willingness of local organisations to respond to changing statutory agendas varies considerably. Some might perceive a seamless fit with their own internal ethos and objectives, and respond with particular projects; for others an element of identity 'repackaging' or 'redefining' might be pursued; some may not respond at all. This chapter will present some examples of how voluntary organisations respond to (or resist) changing agendas. It will illustrate some of their concerns and the dangers inherent in the (sometimes opportunistic) pursuit of new money.

Any discussion of the impacts of the statutory agenda must also consider the mechanisms and processes through which implementation of that agenda is negotiated. This chapter will highlight the increasing political emphasis on statutory/voluntary partnerships – both the opportunities these present, and the difficult coalitions which are formed when this new proximity between the sectors exposes gaps in understanding and confidence. Finally, at the end of a decade characterised by increasing formalisation, by the development of the 'contract culture' and, more recently, the 'compact culture' to define the relationship between the state and the voluntary sector, the case study will also take us behind the scenes to observe the continuing importance of more informal processes and networks for the delivery of statutory objectives.

Introducing the agency: 'Family Friends'

'Family Friends' is a voluntary organisation based in the Midlands, which aims to promote the welfare of families with at least one child under five years of age. Linked volunteers offer regular support, friendship and practical help to families in their own homes, helping to prevent crisis and family breakdown. Half of all referrals are by health visitors and a further quarter come from social workers. Volunteers are carefully selected and trained by the organisers, and are the cornerstone of this work. The bulk of the organisation's funding is from social services – a grant of nearly £100,000 in 1998/99.

The impact of the statutory agenda

In the early and mid-1990s organisations such as this, working with families with young children (outside the field of disability), experienced relatively little growth in their statutory funding. At that time, the political imperative in relation to welfare services was implementation of the community care legislation (see Russell et al, 1995, pp 17-20). However, 'Family Friends' has experienced a precipitous increase in its statutory funding in the last 12 months as a result of recent changes in political priorities – specifically the government's increased emphasis on the family and 'first years', and its longer-term objectives in relation to educational attainment, employment and inclusion.

This has affected the organisation's funding in two ways. First their social services grant has increased by over 30% to around £130,000 for 1999/2000. Second, this £30,000 increase has been matched by funding available through the Department of Education. The increased funding will pay for the appointment of an additional 1.5 workers, and an increase in the number of volunteers to 115, enabling the organisation to extend its work into areas of the city not yet covered. Unlike many opportunities presented by new statutory funding, there has been no distraction of mission here (the 'seamless fit' described earlier). Furthermore, because the

Organisational structure (1998/99)

Board of trustees	Committees	Paid workers	Volunteers
	Finance	Senior organiser	70
	Personnel	3 organisers	
	Child protection	1 project worker	
	Equal opportunities	2 administrators (part time)	
	Strategic planning		

organisation was careful to ensure that costing for the expanded service also included an enhancement of the administrative infrastructure, the capacity of the organisation to absorb the increased workload has been maintained – which is not always possible when voluntary organisations are tempted to pursue new funding to expand or diversify services.

However, Family Friends is also centrally involved in the local implementation of two major new government initiatives – 'Sure Start' and the 'Early Years Partnership'– which will be delivered through local statutory/voluntary sector partnerships. Family Friends' experience of these exemplifies some of the key operational and strategic issues for voluntary organisations involved in responding to statutory agendas:

- the unrealistic time-scales and expectations of policy makers and funders (also illustrated in relation to another initiative at the opening of this chapter);
- the extent to which new funding opportunities can undermine the ethos of the voluntary organisation's working practice and even the viability of the service itself;
- the lack of consultation with voluntary sector 'partners' during the early development of new initiatives, and the imbalance of power within the partnerships themselves;
- the extent to which statutory initiatives and their implementation through multi-agency partnerships have the potential to undermine the identity and self-governance of the individual voluntary organisation.

Time-scales ...

"We knew last year that Sure Start was coming. This is one of the pilot areas, but the plan is that within three years there will be 250 Sure Start projects around the country. It will involve intensive working with families with children under four in an area with a two mile diameter. It is a Dept of Education initiative but Health are also involved. It will have amazing funding. The long-term outcomes the government is looking for are a reduction in exclusion from schools and higher educational attainment levels. They've suddenly come to the realisation that the early years are the important ones, and have come up with Sure Start as the magic solution. Trail Blaze areas were announced on February 9th. Funding

applications had to be with the Sure Start office by March 18th. (Ours was put together by all the partners following a series of meetings, but there was not enough time to debate some of the key issues.) Then a week last Friday (April) we heard that this would be one of the first areas to be funded. This first round of pilot projects were supposed to be active by July – which is madness. The bid for this area was £1 million and the pilot will involve 35 new posts based in different organisations! This is the sort of speed that is expected."

Ethos compromised ...

"I was at a meeting recently where I had this conversation with a worker from a project not unlike ours in the South West. There's this big plan for Sure Start – and it's been planned 'up there' in the local authority. And she was suddenly contacted by them – 'We want your organisation to do the initial assessment visits which are part of the Sure Start programme' and she said 'Yes'! She took the opportunity to create two new posts. So I asked 'Does that make sense in terms of what your project is about? You can't do their assessments on the one hand and still offer a non-judgemental, confidential befriending service on the other – it's changing the culture of what you do'. This problem would perhaps not have arisen had she been consulted during the initial discussions."

The nature of partnership ...

"The local authority has taken the lead role on Sure Start schemes in most areas. Few voluntary organisations have the resources and machinery to do the administration and coordination of these sorts of programmes. Local authorities have that advantage. And of course they work very differently from the voluntary sector. No matter what anyone says, what you find is that they do tend to impose their model of working onto voluntary agencies through the structures and bureaucracies they bring. The Sure Start agency in London are expecting that in each area there will be a board with representatives from all the stake holders on it. The first debate is about the relative numbers from the voluntary and statutory sectors – and who ultimately has the balance of power on the board or how you ensure that there isn't an imbalance. It's like the Early Years Partnership – on the board you not only had officers from individual departments but also members. There were two from everywhere and we were saying: 'Why do you need two from social services, two from education and so on'. Voluntary agencies only had one representative each. Again the voluntary sector is clear that we are not going to participate if there is an imbalance of power. We've lost so many times through this.

"Then under the board there is going to be a Sure Start coordinator. It's not clear who actually employs the coordinator. It can't be the board because as yet this is not a legal entity – it's just a collection of people with an agreement to work together. The same thing is happening with the Early Years Partnership. The local authority do not see that there is an issue: 'Does it really matter?' Well yes; of course it matters. If you're on our side of the fence, it matters a lot!"

Autonomy ...

"There will be all these different workers who will be employed under the Sure Start or Early Years banners – as community workers, home visitors, volunteer coordinators or whatever. They will be coordinated by the Sure Start coordinator, but the posts will actually be commissioned to appropriate agencies. But how can an agency be commissioned to employ a worker to do a particular job, but then have someone who is employed by another agency manage them? They keep saying 'This is working in partnership'. But it isn't. Ultimately it's about the local authority managing people in the voluntary sector. If we can't manage someone who is working here, we are not going to employ them. We as an organisation – our trustees – should be responsible for ensuring that the worker is managed in a way which fits in with the Sure Start ethos, and then our trustees will be responsible to the board. It won't work otherwise – but somehow the local authority want to believe it will work – they want to hold on to ultimate control. We cannot sign partnership documents until these problems have been ironed out."

The voluntary sector: partner or agent?

"You have to be very careful that you don't become an agent of the government. It's not important that we are on the tip of everyone's tongue in local government and central government. What is important is that people see us as an agency that they can come to with confidence for support and not be afraid of using the service. That will not happen if we become too closely 'partnered' with local government. We've got to be really careful about that. We are on a bit of a high at the moment but of course politicians come and go very quickly. And once you have lost the confidence of the people you are working for, it's much harder to get that back than it is to court political favour."

The views and concerns expressed above will be familiar to many in the voluntary sector. In the longer term, however, the political salience of voluntary/statutory partnership working might also have the effect of increasing the potential influence of voluntary agencies over the substance and process of policy development as well as its implementation.

Ideologies defended ...

"As with all these initiatives, the 'stakeholders' as they like to call them are being asked to sign up as partners. Some voluntary organisations have recently refused to sign and support the Early Years Partnership, a programme which will put massive amounts of money from central government into day care. After two years development, at the point where they're going to start appointing staff and setting up new provision, it has just emerged that only day care and play provision which offers sufficient hours to enable parents to return to work will be eligible. This goes right against the philosophy of some organisations which have been involved in developing the initiative locally. The voluntary sector has been drawn into this agenda – expecting that the outcome would be funding to support all types of provision, that what it was all about was parents taking an active interest in their child's future and development and choosing the provision they wanted – but that is not the government's agenda at all. So the local authority is now understandably very frustrated because the money will not be released by central government until these 'partners' have signed up."

A seat at the table: networks, relationships and informal processes

A number of factors will determine the response of the individual agency to the statutory agenda – whether that agenda fits with its own internal aims and objectives or whether the agency is prepared to redefine these; whether it has the organisational capacity to absorb a new area of work or an expansion of its existing work; and – not least – its financial stability and sustainability without the new funding on offer. Separate from these internal organisational characteristics, however, is the wider issue of access.

We suggested in the introduction to this chapter that voluntary organisations operate within a wider organisational 'ecology'. The following narrative (which relates to Family Friends' increased social services funding discussed earlier) illustrates how at the end of a decade concerned with formalising processes for awarding grant aid and purchasing services, the statutory agenda continues to be implemented through a combination of both formal and informal systems. Even as formal systems and processes work towards increased consistency and transparency, information is disseminated to, and access negotiated with, individual voluntary organisations through informal processes determined by past relationships, networks of influence and reputation.

Formal processes ...

"Last year social services announced an across the board cut in voluntary sector funding – just weeks before the end of the financial year. They didn't seem to understand that even a cut of 5% would mean redundancies in some organisations. There was an angry response from voluntary agencies in the city who, for the first time, lobbied collectively. The outcome was the setting up of a subcommittee involving senior politicians, senior officers from all departments and voluntary sector representatives – to establish a corporate strategy on voluntary sector funding. As a result there will be clearer, more open procedures for funding. Everyone will use the same process. Some of the anomalies in the way in which different agencies have been dealt with, which in the past have made people quite angry, will be removed...."

... And informal processes

"The final meeting to put the last details of the corporate strategy together was held in our offices here. After everyone had left, one of the local authority officers who I had known for a long time hung back. I put the kettle on and asked her what it was she wanted to tell me. She replied that 'The Chair wants us to put together costings for extending your service....' She had been called into a meeting with senior members of the council some of whom I knew had long supported this organisation, and of course all this stuff was beginning to come out of central government then about working with families and disaffection and so on, but where this additional money is coming from I don't know. Don't ask me. Meanwhile a number of organisations are being cut. A few have been wiped out completely. I think to myself 'How can I represent the voluntary sector in meetings about cuts while this organisation is getting such an increase.' But it's not about me – or even about this organisation – it's about the political climate nationally now and the emphasis on families."

Conclusions and policy implications

Case study research reveals conflict and ambiguity, contradictory behaviour and differentiated outcomes. We have seen that statutory agendas and processes are not necessarily coherent or consistent, and their impact on individual voluntary agencies will be differentiated by both formal and informal systems of information and access, and a variety of personal, professional and political relationships and networks. While explicit formally agreed processes are to be welcomed, it is important to acknowledge that parallel processes continue; that in many respects these informal processes, whose invisibility raises important questions about inequality and accountability, are often the real 'ball bearings' of statutory policy. Equally the realities of the voluntary sector response to statutory agendas will be complex – and usually less dichotomous either than statements of ideology on the one hand or organisational pragmatism on the other. In practice individual responses will often be a mix of both, and outcomes will be the result of internal and external negotiations. Nevertheless, the experience of the organisation described here does suggest some recommendations for voluntary organisations dependent on statutory funding and subject to the vagaries of political and policy change.

First it is important that organisations should be able to resist funding opportunities where they undermine their ethos or the delivery of existing services:

> "Organisations should have a very clear commitment to pursue independent non-statutory funding. You also need board members with the confidence to say no. This organisation has in fact refused money in the past – which some people feel is very bold. But why? I could maybe understand it if you'd got someone employed, and not having the money meant that person was going to lose their job. But if the job doesn't exist, you are not changing or losing anything. Equally if the funding represents a clear gain, unless you are going to gain something you want, why have it?"

There is a clear need to develop better working relationships between the sectors – genuine participative partnerships and greater mutual understanding so that policy makers and funders can take better account of the capacity and role of voluntary organisations when they are developing policies and programmes.

> "The planning processes should involve independent agencies from day one. We do not have a political mandate but we can advise and inform about the possibilities and constraints. This is what is missing."

> "The partnerships which are being sought involve people with very different organisational cultures, experience and priorities – without the commitment or time to find out about one another. But half the battle is to get acknowledgement that these different perspectives exist. It was completely incomprehensible to one local authority officer for example that you had to nurture volunteers. He thought that 'They come in to do a job don't they? Why do you need to nurture them?'"

One of the ways in which voluntary agencies can begin to resist potentially damaging new funding opportunities is through strategic planning and clarity about their mission.

> "Anticipation is very difficult – it's hard to keep on top – but it is very important to be aware of current research and developments in your field. You can also try to anticipate political changes – you can listen to emerging emphases in public discussion."

> "In terms of buffers – any organisation needs to plan ahead – to have a vision of what it wants to achieve and where it wants to go and you have to go back to that vision every time new opportunities come up – even be prepared to assess whether you want to change your vision. It's very useful to revisit your aims, objectives and ethos. Trustees should be encouraged to do this every year. Too many organisations get so caught up in moving forward, they don't take enough time for reflection."

10

Implications for policy and practice

So what is a 'case study'?

Old French: *casse* – to take or hold

Old French: *cas* – a happening

We can talk of bounded events, happenings within specifically delimited boundaries of place (the corner of a community centre, a neighbourhood, or an organisation) and time (a brief exchange of glances or words, an event, a day, a week or longer). These are the defining characteristics of a form of descriptive research which we would prefer to call 'case histories'. The reader encounters considerable detail about contexts, which is exciting but of limited value in offering wider insights. Explanations and understanding will not simply emerge from the detail.

The extent to which case studies move beyond description depends firstly on the researcher, research relationships and the levels of trust established over time. But the transformation from 'case history' to 'case study' ultimately rests on the extent to which there is also an explicit commitment to analytical frameworks, and their employment not just by the researcher but also to some extent by the informants. Two illustrations of these different, but overlapping approaches, must suffice.

The first is a highly conceptualised set of four studies of voluntary agencies (Christian Aid, Royal National Institute for the Blind, Royal National Lifeboat Institution, and St Dunstans: Butler and Wilson, 1990). We learn much from these about the structures of the sample organisations; there are careful interview schedules which produce tables of correlation coefficients. But the generality of detail hides the processes, the

dynamics, the events, the contradictions. We learn for example, in an almost throwaway line, that there is likely to be:

> ... [an] almost inevitable clash of values between voluntary staff, paid staff and professional managers. (Butler and Wilson, 1990, p 172)

Theirs is a significant taxidermy but, in the last analysis, the butterflies are still pinned to the display board. There is no movement. Case studies, guided by structures, could tell an important part of this story.

A second illustration derives from a set of case studies of government policy making during the past 20 years. Its author concludes that, despite the work of what have come to be called 'spin doctors', there is rarely a coherent and rational explanation behind the twists and turns of state policies In short:

> ... the implied collective single mind is a fiction. (Levin, 1997, p 224)

Furthermore the apparently rigid doctrines of Thatcherism turn out, on closer inspection, to be full of "unspecific aspirations" which allow a "wide range of possibilities for action" (Levin, 1997, p 225). To the extent that these possibilities do develop more or less coherence, the author concludes that this may well result from the behaviour of policy makers as 'emotional' rather than 'rational' actors (Levin, 1997, p 227). If there are important structures which influence policy decisions, these are as likely to be informal as formal, as likely to be ad hoc as prescribed, and as likely to be cross boundary as contained within a single committee or department. Much is made of social policy and practice as existing within "... systems for exerting pressure" (Levin, 1997, p 243).

The fact of there being no single mind, a wide range of possibilities, emotional actors and pressure – these are perhaps a complementary set of 'building bricks' alongside (not necessarily in opposition to) the correlation coefficients of Butler and Wilson. These are two very different analytic approaches to 'case study work', best linked together rather than being offered as polar opposites – for in the words of our second example, "... process and structure are inseparable" (Levin, 1997, p 231).

In this report we have offered eight tentative illustrations of the possibilities of a case study approach to analysing and understanding the real life dilemmas of voluntary organisations. However, experience has taught us that we might also 'draw back the curtain' on events within voluntary agencies, only to find that the truths revealed were still unresolved and inconclusive. In case study research we have to learn to accept social worlds as partially unfinished and opaque. It is nevertheless clear that case studies can open up discussion about key themes central to the sustainability and dynamics of voluntary action, and about inherent contradictions and puzzles, instead of relegating these to hidden places far from the prying eyes of the audit or evaluation.

Perhaps our central conclusion is about the need for voluntary agencies to avoid becoming 'trapped' between the formal tales they tell to the auditor or grant giver, and the informal anecdotes which circulate when the monitoring and evaluation moment has passed. At the most basic level, voluntary agency managers, paid staff and volunteers *and* their colleagues in the statutory sector, need to identify, reflect on and share some of those recurrent 'film strips' of personal or organisational experience which are too frequently hidden away. It is understandable why people tidy up; they wish to appear in control, to be competent and professional, worthy of extra resource or promotion. It is imperative, however, that all those involved in voluntary action build sufficiently trusting relationships that will then encourage them to discuss the realities of voluntary action.

What can we learn from case study work? The policy and practice themes

In spite of the above remarks, about the sometimes unfinished and opaque nature of our findings, we do consider that each issue-based chapter illuminates important policy and practice dilemmas. We present therefore eight brief summaries and accompanying puzzles, which are followed by recommendations.

Infrastructure

It was perhaps not much of a revelation for us to discover that an under-resourced physical and administrative environment has implications for organisational effectiveness and sustainability. But it was a little more surprising to discover within one small local agency, almost entirely peopled by volunteers, how far different, and sometimes contradictory, perspectives about infrastructure existed. Indeed these same tensions were expressed even by individual informants.

On the one hand people were proud of the fact that they could do a lot with a little; after all, isn't that what the 'real' voluntary sector is all about? Yet at the same time, people were aware of the consequences of false economies – inadequate training support or maintenance programmes for relatively expensive workers and equipment for example. Not all of these dilemmas or contradictions could be explained away via references to 'if only we had the money'. Key catalysts were the experiences and reflections of the two part-time workers. They were the transmission belts or conduits for bigger, non-local influences about the need for a more effective physical and social infrastructure. Yet, even as they attempted to rise above their local constraints (the room, telephone, toilet, filing cabinet, table, letter box), so these efforts might in the longer term unconsciously put at risk the accessible, cheap social infrastructure which had produced them.

Recommendations

The development of new physical (and social) infrastructure cannot be introduced without sensitive regard for existing coping strategies. Many subtle local reciprocities have grown out of bartering for space, second-hand furniture, training and the like. When the office equipment catalogue replaces these, important relationships may be displaced. Close observation, even of privation, is therefore necessary before changes are introduced. Nevertheless funding agencies, and statutory purchasers who rely on voluntary organisations to provide basic local services, should also recognise their infrastructure needs as a legitimate cost.

Values and identity

The sheer variety of voluntary action – its different purposes and organisations – guarantees a comparable richness in terms of values and identities. But if one single focus for value/ identity issues exists, this must centre on the so-called 'voluntary' motivation of the vast majority of people involved. It is clear that the influences which prompt initial volunteering, continuing involvement and eventual exit are often much less rational than surveys might suggest, and that sustaining voluntary commitment will always be a delicate activity which varies between organisations.

We chose Health Self Help to illustrate some of the complexity and contradictions just because it was small and entirely voluntary. It became clear that notions of altruism, duty and obligation were rooted in both personal history and interpersonal relations. Furthermore, these notions or values were neither absolute not static; they were negotiated with others and seemed highly contingent on a sense of identity which changed over time.

Recommendations

It is tempting to suggest that voluntary organisations should 'monitor' or 'audit' the changing values and identity of their volunteers – particularly those who hold key positions. Unfortunately, these terms have acquired a particular formal meaning and their very mention may cause resistance in many agencies. What is clear is that much informal social life depends on processes of mutual appraisal which are similar to the more regulatory emphases of monitoring and audits. 'How are you?' can therefore be more than an empty ritual; at least on an annual basis, those responsible for the maintenance of voluntary organisations should identify and celebrate the values and identities of their

volunteers. If they forget to do this, people may exit in ways which are potentially damaging.

The processes of identification and celebration need not be solely a matter for the individual agency or its active core. In a world where many occupations and professions hold 'awards ceremonies' and distribute 'Life Time Achievement' certificates, it is not inappropriate to recognise and reward local volunteers on an annual basis. Volunteer bureaux can play a part, alongside volunteer development staff within health authorities and social service departments.

Social entrepreneurs

The term 'social entrepreneur' has been introduced in relation to the voluntary sector in the 1990s without sufficient analysis. The entrepreneur was clearly a much lauded role in the private market economy of the 1980s but the prefix 'social' raises general and particular questions.

In the first place, social entrepreneurs appear to be exceptionally active and socially skilful 'go-betweens' within and between voluntary agencies as well as other institutions such as local government and industry. But, does this activity and skill operate with equal effectiveness across the whole landscape of horizontal and vertical divisions?

Secondly what are the personal and organisational 'costs' of a fuzzily defined activity? (Indeed it may well be an advantage, at least initially, for entrepreneurs to be imprecisely located!) The self-taught, non-stop champion might come to feel a mistake-laden, burnt out failure.

Recommendations

Entrepreneurship is often very context-specific; it is important to support and develop more general forms which can be used across contexts. Beware the cult of the 'Superwoman'. Social entrepreneurs need formal and informal support before they believe their own propaganda that they can 'fix' everything. Organisations must try to avoid over-reliance and take succession planning seriously; it may require 12 months of (ir)regular discussions to move from one social entrepreneur to another; it may be helpful to appoint junior and senior social entrepreneurs to ease succession; it may be possible to share social entrepreneurs (and their support/succession) between agencies. Here intermediary agencies (such as the CVS [Council of Voluntary Service] and RCC [Rural Community Council]) can be helpful.

Stakeholders

Stakeholders are the different faces, or different interests, of voluntary organisations. Often these differences are not fully recognised or understood by analysts, by funders or by users – or indeed by voluntary organisations themselves. Stakeholding is generally presented as a positive concept, implying both investment and empowerment. Yet in practice the different interests of different stakeholders can be contradictory or conflicting. This is particularly the case where some stakeholders are more powerful, or perceive themselves to be more powerful, than others.

The agendas set by key funders, both from the voluntary and statutory sectors, are clear examples of stakeholders wielding power. And sometimes this is done in a fashion which leaves others feeling that their interests have been ignored or over-ridden. Investment and empowerment are replaced by exclusion and dis-empowerment, which undermine rather than promote stakeholding. Different stakeholders may not always agree with each other, or be equally at ease with all developments; but if they are excluded from knowledge about, or involvement in, such developments, then the stake they hold may become worthless to them – and to the organisation in which they hold it. Stakeholders grow and decay to the extent that their contributions are valued and nurtured.

Recommendations

Stakeholders may be of equal worth – in an intrinsic sense – but their different individual origins, experience, and competence will lead to differential behaviour and expectations. Gender, age, class and ethnicity are just some of the fault lines to be overcome. Over-laying these differences will be the more structural inequalities of intraagency and interagency contexts. The first task of agencies is to identify these individual differences and structural fault lines. Then and only then attention should be paid to:

- the potential and limits of information and consultation – stakeholding can be enhanced to some extent if there is a democracy of information;
- the inevitability and management of dissent – every stakeholder need not always agree but there have to be recognised mechanisms for disagreement, truces and new beginnings; merely sticking the label 'stakeholder' on old wounds can do more harm than good.

Managerialism

New public management approaches can improve organisational practice and service delivery, but they can also have deleterious consequences for voluntary organisations. New management systems, for example, can fragment organisational structure. Vertical demarcation is introduced between different tasks and areas of activity; horizontal demarcation is inserted between different levels of responsibility and power. Tighter individual management can mean looser individual commitment and the eventual development of a 'jobsworth' culture of bureaucracy and buck-passing. Such a loss of commitment and flexibility is not just a practical problem within voluntary organisations; it is a blow to their fundamental ethos – and once lost may not be easy to reclaim.

These organisational divisions also create differential perceptions of managerialism, as commonly found in public agencies too. For those (now) at the top, new practices are a 'challenge' to be met, with problems to be overcome; for others the consequences may become a 'burden' to be shouldered with ever-increasing concern.

Recommendations

Those voluntary organisations which are relatively large and have complex operational structures clearly have particular management needs. Insofar as managerialism becomes distorted into a belief that all or most organisational problems can be resolved through generalised formal procedures, then the problem becomes one of interpretation and application rather than the principle of management per se.

The challenge for managerialism is when to 'let go' – when to recognise that the resolution of some problems must take account of the particular needs and capacities of workers and volunteers as well as service users, and that these may be shaped by different values and frameworks than those associated with managerial priorities and perspectives. In the end, effective managers are people who are not only aware of the limits of their own knowledge and authority but also recognise the equally legitimate width and depth of contributions from workers, volunteers and users.

Strategic planning

There is no shortage of advisors and consultants who wish to promote strategic planning; the worry is that this happens without due regard for organisational contexts and longer-term consequences.

Strategic planning is therefore frequently a one-off event (for example, an 'away day') or an outcome (perhaps a paper-based framework), rather than a process with roots in the everyday life of an organisation. But everyday life is full of unwelcome contingencies, prompted by external forces as well as the unpredictable trajectories of internal groups and individuals. The best strategic plans avoid straitjackets, allow as much room for the people as for the plan, and accept that incompleteness is not synonymous with incompetence and inefficiency.

Recommendations

Strategic plans should build into their structure and content clearly outlined and costed details for the 'predictable unexpected'. Some analogies might be the car breakdown and trouble at sea; it is rarely possible to anticipate the timing and exact circumstances of these events but some preparations (tool kits, life jackets) and practices (changing the wheel on the drive, lessons in the local swimming pool) can help. There should also be provision in voluntary sector training and supervision programmes for responses to the unexpected. For example, it has been an annual occurrence for decades that government agencies will suddenly launch new funding programmes with impossible lead times. Staff meetings, away days and the like should practice 'real time' and 'slow motion' sessions in anticipation of at least one significant 'unpredictable' per annum.

Networking

Networks are not all the same. They have different structures and different purposes. Networking is also a cumulative activity; involvement in networks has to be built up over time. It is a product of informal as well as formal activity, and it encompasses individual relationships (even friendships) as well as formal organisational links. The fact that network relationships can be personal as well as institutional raises questions about who within an organisation should be involved in networking. The answer is not always clear, and there is an overlap here with issues of social entrepreneurship and strategic planning.

Networks are inclusive relationships, but more formally constituted networks can also be exclusive. Some organisations, and some people, are in or out. For those who are out, getting in (or getting back in) can be difficult or impossible. Networking is a process, not an outcome. Thus networks, and membership of them, must be worked at consistently and with commitment; organisations may even have to be prepared to shift allegiances as circumstances, or people, change. It is also not clear to what extent membership of networks is a 'positional' good. To some extent it clearly is – if one organisation is to benefit in achieving a grant or a contract from the knowledge and contacts it has established through networking, then inevitably this means that other organisations may lose out. However, networking is not always so exclusive; indeed many networks are strengthened by a growth in the breadth, and depth, of their membership. This makes issues of who can and cannot be involved in networks, and what different participants get out of them, all the more complex – and all the more important.

Recommendations

The role of networks in the life of voluntary organisations is not necessarily marginal or faintly clandestine as sometimes characterised. In fact networks are often so important that they should be explicitly recognised in:

- annual monitoring and reporting;
- training and support;
- the systems of individual, group and agency accountability;
- strategic planning, project design and funding applications.

External agendas

Most voluntary organisations make much of their independence while experiencing an almost daily struggle with the demands and expectations of external agencies, and the opportunities these might afford. Even those with little outside income are acutely aware of the frequently divergent activities of others. For those agencies with significant levels of statutory funding, it is increasingly evident that external agendas are now a major, often dominant, factor.

Partnership relationships are supposed to resolve misunderstanding and tension; but such arrangements are frequently cosmetic devices designed to secure additional sums of money quickly. Superficially conceived and inadequately resourced, they can fall victim to impossible expectations.

Recommendations

External agendas should be legitimately resisted, whenever voluntary organisations perceive them to be potentially harmful. This is obviously risky as sponsors are normally to be courted rather than rejected and the further development of local compacts must recognise penalty free disengagement.

At the same time it is clear that all parties need to recognise the subtle, often invisible, pressures which shape individual and collective behaviour. External agendas are not always limited to the words on a page; they just as often refer to assumptions and inclinations which are never written down. At least three of our chapters (Strategic planning, Networking, External agendas) reveal the significance of the intra- and interorganisational ecology within which voluntary organisations and local government departments work and interact. These cannot be hidden away in the metaphorical Agenda Bs of institutional life – they are to be recognised and explored, at least in general terms.

A word about Procrustes

Procrustes was a figure in Greek mythology. He robbed travellers and put them in his bed, stretching or cutting off limbs to make their bodies fit. His name comes from a Greek word meaning to extend, by hammering out. Many of us are Procrustean – we want to fit the world into our frameworks, often regardless of the damage this might do. Whether as policy makers, politicians or researchers, it is often more convenient to round things off, to avoid awkward detail.

In the particular context of voluntary – statutory sector relationships, practitioners may feel 'stretched out' on the Procrustean audit bed. Policy makers, however, are often as worn down as the next person by the growing (Procrustean) emphasis on an audit and inspection culture. These case studies are offered as stepping stones away from such an emphasis, towards a more confident acceptance of the everyday fabric of voluntary action. We hope that the vignettes and commentary in this report signal the legitimacy of contradictory experience and encourage ways of both celebrating and exploring it. We talked in Chapter 1 about telescopes and microscopes. The glass-based imagery may have been a little too ambitious; too precise and scientific for the elusive social realities before us. Perhaps we may now speak of our case studies acting like an old mirror – an incomplete mix of cracks and silvered clarity. Much will depend on how it is held and where people stand. We hope some new light will be shed on the people and the processes, on the informal and formal dimensions of their work.

All who wish to understand voluntary action will need to balance the parochialism of the case study approach against its attention to process and dynamics. Dense, located detail, critically analysed, is as important as thinner, if numerically significant, statistical outputs. This is a message for all who study voluntary organisations, whether as policy makers, practitioners, researchers or students.

References

Alcock, P., Harrow, J., Macmillan, R., Vincent, J. and Pearson, S. (1999) *Making funding work: Funding regimes and local voluntary organisations*, York: York Publishing Services.

Burgess, H. (1985) 'Case-study and curriculum research: some issues for teacher researchers', in R. Burgess (ed) *Issues in educational research: Qualitative methods*, Lewes: Falmer.

Butler, R.J. and Wilson, D.C. (1990) *Managing voluntary and non-profit organisations: Strategy and structure*, London: Routledge.

Elsdon, K. (1991) *Adult learning in voluntary organisations, Volume 1*, Nottingham: University of Nottingham.

Glaser, B. and Strauss, A. (1967) *The discovery of grounded theory: Strategies for qualitative research*, Chicago, IL: Aldine.

Hammersley, M. (1992) 'So what are the case studies', *What's wrong with ethnography?*, London: Routledge, ch 11.

Hammersley, M. and Atkinson, P. (1996) *Ethnography: Principles in practice*, London: Routledge.

Hart, C., Jones, K. and Bains, M. (1997) 'Do people want power? The social responsibilities of empowering communities', in P. Hoggett (ed) *Contested communities: Experiences, struggles, policies*, Bristol: The Policy Press, pp 180-200.

Heath, J. (1999) 'How to get more out of case studies', *Times Higher Education Supplement*, 12 February.

Hoggett, P. (ed) (1997) *Contested communities: Experiences, struggles, policies*, Bristol: The Policy Press.

Levin, P. (1997) *Making social policy: The mechanisms of government and politics, and how to investigate them*, Buckingham: Open University Press.

O'Connor, T. (1994) *Birth to five: The establishment of Childline*, Case Study 7, CVO, London: London School of Economics.

Plummer, K. (1983) *Documents of life: An introduction to the problems and literature of a humanistic method*, London: Allen & Unwin.

Reynolds, J., Elsdon, K.T. and Stewart, S. (1994) *A town in action: Voluntary networks in Retford*, Nottingham: Department of Adult Education, University of Nottingham.

Ritchie, C., Taket, A. and Bryant, J. (1994) *Community works: 26 case studies showing community operational research in action*, Sheffield: Sheffield Hallam University Press.

Rochester, C. (1999) *Building the capacity of small voluntary agencies: Juggling on a unicycle – A handbook for small voluntary organisations*, CVO, London: London School of Economics.

Rochester, C., Harris, J. and Hutchinson, R. (1999) *Building the capacity of small voluntary agencies, Final Report*, CVO, London: London School of Economics.

Russell, L. and Scott, D. (1997) *Very active citizens? The impact of the contract culture on volunteers*, Manchester: University of Manchester.

Russell, L., Scott, D. and Wilding, P. (1995) *Mixed fortunes. The funding of the voluntary sector*, Manchester: University of Manchester.

Sanger, J. (1996) *The complete observer? A field research guide to observation*, Lewes: Falmer.

Smith, P. (1995) *The challenge of partnership: A study of the relationship between City Challenge and the voluntary sector in one London borough*, Case Study 9, CVO, London: London School of Economics.

Stake, R.E. (1995) *The art of case study research*, Thousand Oaks: Sage Publications.

Vittles, P. (1999) *An overview of qualitative research techniques*, Unpublished paper given at 'Beyond statistics: The role of qualitative research in the new local government agenda', Conference organised by the Scottish Local Government Information Unit at Stirling, 7 September.

Yin, R. (1994) *Case study research: Design and methods*, Newbury Park: Sage Publications.